IN THE PALMS OF HIS HANDS
A Journey Toward Home

by
Andrea Stefanovik

xulon PRESS

www.xulonpress.com

TO

My husband, Miroljub: Thank you for being my prayer partner, my encourager, and my best friend. Thank you for listening to our Lord and Savior, and for being obedient to His instructions, and thank you for challenging me to grow in ways I never imagined.

My dear friend, Claudia Ryan: I want to thank you for being my friend and sister in Christ. I would not have been able to put this together without your prayers, support, and encouragement. You are a true friend and sister for life.

PREFACE

This book has been written with much prayer and encouragement. It has been written with the hope that it will touch the hearts of readers and cause them to become aware of how much God is in control of our lives, even during our most difficult times. As the Bible says, He has known us from the time of conception (Jeremiah 1:5). He has counted every hair on our heads from the beginning of time. He has a plan and a purpose for our lives. Now He waits with open arms for us to respond to His invitation of love. He never promises us lives without pain and suffering, but He does promise to get us through those times victoriously, until one day we can stand before Him and He can say, "Well done, good and faithful servant...."

My desire is for the reader to see the purpose of their life and to see God's supportive hand in every area, even in those places where we think we have failed. Once the purpose is recognized, my desire is to see the reader live for God in full surrender to Him to fulfill the destiny God has planned for that life.

Our lives are unpredictable and we do not always have control over the things that come our way, but we do have a choice as to whom we will serve. God never promised it would be without a price. He did, however, promise to bring us through every situation. With the Lord, we can know that nothing is by happenstance, but that there is a mighty hand at work in everything. Our Lord sees everything that happens to us. He never leaves nor forsakes us. Everything that happens in our lives is designed to give God glory though our testimony. I gave my life to Jesus when I was nineteen years old, but I only began to understand the true walk at the age of twenty-six. I realized then that there was more to God and this Christian walk than I imagined. Although the road would be full of more lessons and hurts, once I tasted the sweetness of what it really meant to live for Him, I could not get enough. The Bible came alive, and my life became purpose-driven.

My desire is to bring Him glory and honor, and I want nothing more than to serve Him with all my heart, soul, mind, and strength. May the rest of my life be used mightily for Him, and may He fulfill all His purposes within me and through me. There is absolutely nothing more satisfying in this life than to live for God and be in His Will.

I pray that this book will open the reader's eyes and cause all who read it to dig deeper into God's Word to know His will. We are only here for a short time, so let this life be a living testimony for our Lord, Jesus Christ.

Andrea Stefanovik

CONTENTS

CHAPTER ONE
FIGHT FOR FREEDOM

Was it a dream or was it reality? Whatever it was, I wanted it to end quickly. I can remember one snowy day, sitting in the dirt-floored kitchen next to a wood-burning stove on a little stool looking at the front door, waiting for someone to burst in. I was watching the door like a soldier in combat, waiting to run for cover in case of an attack. I remember rocking and singing some unknown tune in my head, trying to comfort myself in that dark, cold, and lonely kitchen. I was a five-year-old messy, dirty, confused little girl, and I was all alone in an old, damp, musty home in a village in northeast Hungary.

As I intently watched outside, I saw someone in a white hat. I heard talking and someone calling out my name.

"Andrea, open the door. It's your mother."

I knew better than to respond. I had been told that my mother was a witch and to be ready to run from her in case she came for me. I was not about to open the door. To me, she was a stranger.

But the knocking and calling did not stop; instead, it intensified. All of a sudden, the door flew open with a huge crack. It broke off the hinge, and pieces went flying everywhere. Then I saw a strange man in a leather coat beside this woman who identified herself as my mother. The woman grabbed me, and I began kicking and screaming, begging her not to take me away. Next, I saw my grandmother running in our direction. She was returning from the field. She pushed her way in, and in an attempt to rescue me from the hands of these strangers, she grabbed a knife and went after the man. But she was overcome by his strength. As he threw her up against the wall, the knife flew out of her hands. Meanwhile, I was being forcefully carried down the driveway in the direction of a running car with a racing engine that was ready to make haste at any moment. Another unknown man was waiting eagerly in it, running the engine, waiting for the signal. Cautiously, but with a stern force, my mother pushed me into the car and we drove off, never again to turn back. After three years of court cases and rescue attempts, a new chapter in my life was about to begin, but it would not be easy or trouble-free.

I was born in 1967 in Tatabonya, Hungary, during the time when Hungary was under the control of the communists. Fortunately, I do remember a significant portion of my life. I say fortunately because I have come to believe that our memories serve as an ointment of healing. I can remember all the way back to when I was five years old, and perhaps younger. My mother's experiences were conveyed to me by her and family members who knew the situation well. They told me what we went through to obtain the freedom we now had, spiritually and physically. However, the battle for custody had all been documented in the courts as far up as the Supreme Court of Hungary. My experiences were embedded in my mind from the time I was taken from my mother, and they are as real to me today as they were at the time they were taking place. This is a child's look back at the tragic problems of what family rivalries can cause and what long-term effects they can have on an innocent child. However, looking back also reveals the fact and truth that I was never alone. Although I did not understand why I was not rescued from these tragedies, I could see later in life that they contributed to the shape of my very existence. How they shape us can be determined by how we react. In our own strength, we can do nothing, but with God, all things are possible (Matthew 19:26). That is the reality of life.

My mother grew up in a village located about an hour away from the capital. She was the second youngest girl of six children. Perhaps she thought that if she did not get married soon, she would be trapped in time. Perhaps she felt cheated because when it came time for her to further her education, her parents could not afford to send her and her younger brother to school. Therefore, based on the customs at that time, they chose to send her younger brother, which left her home alone with aging parents.

My mother finally got her chance to leave home when she met her future husband, my father. Shortly after their marriage, the excitement of new life filled the air. However, all the excitement was soon overshadowed by the reality of my father's true personality. Apparently, my father had a drinking problem, which then resulted in an abusive marriage. The lies soon began to be exposed as my mother found out that even the army did not want to keep him due to his habitual drinking. Abuse soon became the norm in their home, and my mother decided she needed to make some drastic changes. Just before she was due to deliver me, her first and only child, my father kicked her in the stomach, which almost caused her to miscarry. Nevertheless, she was able to rush herself to the hospital in time to receive treatment to prevent the miscarriage. She delivered a healthy baby girl on April 18, 1967.

Our right to live is predestined by our God, and only He is justified to take it away. I was spared that day because God Almighty was in control of the situation. He confirms that to us in Jeremiah 1:4-5, 29:11:

The word of the Lord came to me, saying, "Before I formed you in the womb, I knew you, before you were born I set you apart...."
"For I know the plans I have for you," declares the Lord, "plans to prosper you and not to harm you, plans to give you hope and a future."

When we are young, we may not understand how God works, but if our eyes are opened, time will prove His intervention and power in controlling the situation. The Bible says that He knew us before we were formed in our mother's womb and He has already counted all the hairs on our heads. He has a plan and a destiny for our lives and nothing can stop His plan. This means that nothing goes unnoticed, and we should take comfort in knowing that no action by man can change that. He will use the good and the bad in our lives to fulfill His purpose, even when we are unable to speak for ourselves:

> *In Him we were also chosen, having been predestined according to the plan of Him who works out everything in conformity with the purpose of His will.*
>
> *Ephesians 1:11*

My mother said that the situation became so unbearable with my father that she wanted to die. In her frantic desperation, she tried to take her own life by turning on the gas stove, but after what I believe was a serious mental battle within, she could not go through with it. The knowledge of this attempt left its mark on my heart and mind forever.

As I grew up and learned about this attempt, it bothered me that she would hold on to me with that amount of intensity. In contemplating suicide, she was protecting herself and preventing my father from taking me. Perhaps she saw it as love; I saw it as possession. Perhaps she saw it as preventing me from experiencing future pain and suffering; I saw it as an act of selfishness and control. After she shared that with me, I decided to keep a safe distance from her, mentally and physically. This added to the problematic relationship she and I were already experiencing as I was coming of age. For a long time, I could not shake the thought of her deciding to end my life. Was this decision hers to make? I could not speak for myself at that age, but I thank God that He filled her with enough guilt to stop her. I believe she was not wrong in sharing this with me, but I needed to pray for the healing of this wound in me and forgive my mother so the sins of the mother would not be visited on the child.

Finally, when I was about three years old, my mother decided that her only choice was divorce. She was forced to enter into the court system in order to gain custody of me. My father was granted visitation rights, but with strict rules. One of the rules was that my father had to notify my mother when he was coming for me. One day, he deliberately failed to follow the rules. He told my grandmother that he had permission from my mother to come and take me for the day. So, without hesitation, but with much ignorance, I was handed over to him. That was the last time my mother would see me for three years. I wondered if, at that moment, she regretted not going through with the suicide attempt.

Unlike a democratic country where you are considered innocent until proven guilty, communism shows no favoritism or mercy. You are guilty until proven innocent, and Hungary was no exception.

Once the court decided that my mother was to have full custody of me, they did not hesitate to offer to use full force in order to get me back. My mother was told that they would have to give my father a chance to return me, and if he did not do so willingly, then the courts would intervene by using the police. However, my mother was reluctant, knowing the kind of force the police would use and the emotional impact it would have on me. She knew they would not hesitate to use weapons should my father not cooperate. Therefore, she pleaded with the Judge to allow her to get me back. She knew she could not make the journey alone, but she shared her plans with the Judge. Off the record, the Judge told her to do whatever she felt she had to in order to rescue me.

My mother first went to the men in her family to ask them if they were willing to help her. To her amazement, they were not willing. Perhaps her family did not believe her story about the Judge approving her actions. They also had families to consider, and they did not want to cause any bad waves with the government. So they all decided to decline the invitation.

As time passed, my mother met a man that would find the search and rescue rather challenging and exciting. The unknown has a way of grabbing those who are always out to find new excitement with which to fill their empty lives. He was not only willing to go along with her, but also willing to marry her to keep the courts from having any reason to object to her having full custody of me. Years later, my mother confessed that one of the reasons she married my stepfather was to use him for the rescue. In those days, single mothers were not thought of very highly. However, what was that teaching me?

I was a child caught between two parents, each with their own motives and agendas. There would be a total of three rescue attempts before one would succeed. I cannot help but see the hand of God even in the number of times they attempted to get me back. Interestingly, the number three is a holy number. It represents the Trinity—the Father, the Son, and the Holy Spirit. The number three is also associated with the resurrection, divine completeness, and perfection in the Bible (Vallowe, pg. 53. 1998).

The first attempt: I remember a considerable amount of this first trip since it involved so much fear. For a young child, it was an attempt to get away from the monster "in the closet" that tried to get to us while we slept. I remember my grandmother telling me we had to go for a walk because the witch was coming for me. We walked a long time in the woods. We would follow the stream near our home. They did not tell me why they were taking me there, but said that we had to hide, otherwise I would never see them again. I remember the indescribable fear that came over me. I did not like being there, and I did not like the other children in the village. I remember how abusive they were towards me. They would bully me and physically force me to do things that would sow fear and distrust in me later in life. Perhaps they made fun of me for who I was because they knew that I really did not belong, or as with most kids, they just wanted to see how far they could go.

The second attempt: This attempt involved more physical contact. It was an unforgettable scene. My mother and her two companions managed to make it up the driveway without being seen. However, one of the neighbors saw my mother looking into the house and heard her calling out my name. The neighbor fetched my grandmother from the field, but by the time she came home, my mother already had me in her arms. I was usually left home alone while my father went to work and my grandmother took the cows into the pasture.

In her desperate attempt to help me, my grandmother grabbed my feet and a game of tug-of-war began. I screamed and yelled for my grandmother to not let me go. And then, a mother's worst nightmare came true—I hollered as loud as I could for my grandmother not to let the 'witch' take me. My mother was left to make a choice: pull until she dislocated my limbs, or let go and leave brokenhearted. She chose the latter. I cannot even attempt to understand what she must have been feeling at that moment. If it's true that during the early stages of childhood the bond that forms between a child and a mother is strong, then she must have felt like a piece of her own body was being torn away from her. Not to mention what she must have felt when she heard me call her a 'witch' instead of 'mom.' My mother proved her love for me as her child by letting go. I was the one caught in the middle. I was mentally and physically unable to make a decision.

I am reminded of the story in First Kings when Solomon used his God-given wisdom to decide which woman was the real mother of a poor, innocent child who just happened to be in the wrong place at the wrong time. Solomon decided that the only way to resolve the conflict was to literally cut the child in two. At that moment, the real mother spoke up immediately and withdrew her hands in order to save the child's life. The story went as follows:

Now two prostitutes came to the king and stood before him. One of them said, "My Lord, this woman and I live in the same house. I had a baby while she was there with me. The third day after my child was born, this woman also had a baby. We were alone; there was no one in the house but the two of us. "During the night this woman's son died because she lay on him. So she got up in the middle of the night and took my son from my side while I your servant was asleep. She put him by her breast and put her dead son by my breast. The next morning, I got up to nurse my son—and he was dead! But when I looked at him closely in the morning light, I saw that it wasn't the son I had borne." The other woman said, "No! The living one is my son; the dead one is yours." But the first one insisted, "No! The dead one is yours; the living one is mine." And so they argued before the king. The king said, "This one says, 'My son is alive and your son is dead,' while that one says, 'No! Your son is dead and mine is alive.'" Then the king said, "Bring me a sword." So they brought a sword for the king. He then gave an order: "Cut the living child in two and give half to one and half to the other." The woman whose son was alive was filled with compassion for her son and said to the king, "Please, my Lord, give her the living baby! Don't kill him!" But the other said, "Neither I nor you shall have him. Cut him in two!" Then the king gave his ruling: "Give the living baby to the first woman. Do not kill him; she is his mother."

1 Kings 3:16-27

In the same way, my mother let go of me in order to prevent any further mental or physical pain.

Later in life, when I knew the love of God and His love for me, I thought back to that moment and what my mother must have felt. Could it be that was how our Father in heaven felt when His Son Jesus was being beaten and crucified? Could it be when Jesus gave up His Spirit that the rain that began falling over Jerusalem was the tear of the Father crying for His Son? Crying that He had to go through so much pain and so much rejection in order to destroy the power of death forever, in order to have a family and a bride? Crying because He was forced to turn His back on His only begotten in order to once again give access into the Holy of Holies to the entire world? I wonder... and the best part is that it was all a gift to those who are open to accept it.

For God so loved the world that he gave his one and only Son, that whoever believes in him shall not perish but have eternal life. For God did not send his Son into the world to condemn the world, but to save the world through him.

John 3:16-17

My mother later told me that she could not believe how much my father and his family had brainwashed me. When she saw how scared I was to go with her, she could not take the pain. But that reality gave her the determination to rescue me from that lifestyle and abuse.

The third attempt: God's intervention would be the last attempt. This time, a neighbor in the town where I lived (Telkibanya) decided to help my mother. This neighbor saw the awful conditions I lived in and knew that my mother would offer me a better life. Perhaps she was the one who told my grandmother they were coming the first time, and now the guilt of seeing the truth was tormenting her. She was keeping a very close watch on the family's movements. Since my father's twin brothers worked for this neighbor's husband, she knew their work schedules, and she knew when the house was safe for my mother to approach. The neighbor agreed to cooperate and to contact my mother when the time was right.

Finally, the day came and my mother, her new husband, and their friend were ready. The neighbor told them to park the car in the center of the town and walk up to her house as if they were her guests. They left for Telkibanya, drove all night, and arrived the following day at dawn. They left the car where they were told and began to walk up to the neighbor's house. As they were walking, they could not believe their eyes when they saw my grandfather walking towards them, headed towards the train station. As was custom in most small towns, they greeted each other as old acquaintances and good neighbors should. They kept walking with a slight tremble in their spirit as they covered themselves with the hope that they would not be recognized.

My mother found out later that he was headed to file another appeal for custody. My father and his family knew the system well. The appeals kept the case in an ongoing status that allowed them to keep me longer while they planned to come up with a final solution that would prevent me from ever seeing my mother again.

As my mother looked back, she noticed that my grandfather was also looking back at them. He must have felt something was wrong, but praised God for His blinding powers. God is in control and He has the power and authority to blind and give sight. It reminded me of Lot and the time when the angels blinded the men in the town so that they could escape from the city of Sodom. God made a way of escape and spared their lives. He gave them instructions to never look back, and it was up to them to choose whom they would listen to that day. The ones that listened to God were spared, but the ones that chose to turn back were destroyed (Gen. 19).

This trip was during the winter season, and that particular day was very cold. As they walked, their feet were beginning to feel the effects of the weather. Their journey was not going to be easy. The harshness of the weather and the excitement of the event made the short walk seem like an eternity. Everything seemed to be moving in slow motion. Everyone was quiet and eager with anticipation. They finally made it to the neighbor's house, and now all they could do was wait. They had to wait for everyone to leave my father's house before they would be able to go back, get the car, and proceed with their plan of escape.

The neighbor's husband had also decided to cooperate. Therefore, this particular morning, he scheduled my father and his twin brothers work in a different location so they would not pass by the car and recognize it. As my mom and the neighbor watched through a small window in the kitchen, they saw them leave one by one, and finally, my grandmother left for the field. But this time, they noticed that I was not with her. They started getting nervous since the plan was to take me from my grandmother as she and I walked to the creek. Now they did not know where I was. They had no choice but to assume I was still in the house. My mother told her friend to go get the car, bring it up to the house, and open the hood as if there was a problem—but to keep the car running. She was going to the house to see if I was in there.

At that moment, my mother decided that it was a now or never situation. This was the day, and she was not willing to wait any longer. She went around the house and approached the door. As she knocked, she peeked in through a small crack and saw me sitting on a small stool in the dirt-floored kitchen, shaking and rocking with fear.

I remember that day very clearly. I heard her call out my name and ask me to open the door. She identified herself as my mother. But I would not move. I could not move. I was frozen with fear and trembling. In the meantime, another neighbor that did not like my mother ran and told my grandmother that my mother came for me. As my mother began to walk away to get some help, she noticed in the distance that my grandmother was coming back from the field. She saw her put the cows in the barn and head to the house. She and my stepfather immediately decided to go back to the house and force their way in. She got to the door and told my grandmother to bring me out because she wanted to see me. As she peeked in again, she noticed that my grandmother was holding me and telling me to be quiet. By now, almost the entire town was awake and watching the event unfold. They all watched from a distance because they were too frightened and divided over the situation to get involved.

My grandmother refused to open the door. My mother said she felt a surge of power enter her, and she was so filled with rage at that point that she suddenly turned, and with all the strength within her, slammed her body into the door, only to be tossed back by the aftershock. The door stayed shut. She turned around, and without hesitation, she slammed into it again. This time, the door gave with such force that pieces of it flew everywhere. My mother ran in, pushed my grandmother, and forcefully grabbed me out of her arms. She did not expect me to be as heavy as I was or to put up a fight like I did. She didn't realize how much I had grown from the last time she saw me. But she just held on and ran towards the running car.

That was when my grandmother grabbed a knife and headed after us. At that point, contrary to the court's advice, my step-father had no choice but to get involved, so he pushed my grandmother against the wall to force her to drop the knife. He had succeeded in stalling her long enough to give us time to make it to the car. But she was not about to give up that easily.

With a sigh of relief and a screaming child, we drove off. The car was old and slow, and all the extra weight did not help the speed, but it was all we had. As we turned to take one more look, we noticed that everyone who saw the exciting event unfold came out of their homes and were clapping and waving to us as we drove away. They were happy to see my mom succeed, yet they did not want to help. When you see someone in need, it would be wise to not turn your back on them. You could find yourself in the same position one day and wonder why no one is willing to lend a hand.

We were all brought back to reality quickly as, to our surprise, we suddenly heard a terrible noise behind the car. We realized that my grandmother somehow caught up to us, grabbed the bumper of the car, and was holding on. So much for speed....

Without hesitation, my mother commanded the driver to keep going and press on the pedal as hard as he could. They did not want to hurt her, but to stop meant to give up and start all over again. He forcefully stepped on the gas and caused her to fall. From a distance, she seemed to be unhurt because she got up and waved her fist at us in anger and defeat.

Just as we were approaching the end of town, we were forced to stop at the railroad crossing. Trains in Hungary were very long and took quite a while to get across the road. This particular train however had someone special on it—my grandfather. They could not believe their eyes as they looked up and saw him looking right back at them. They decided to roll the window down and wave to him, knowing they were safe since he would dare not jump off a moving train. Knowing there was nothing he could do, he ran back and forth in the train car to get another glimpse, and with a sigh, his face finally showed the agony of defeat.

My earthly father did not provide a home for me. He was not raising me in a nurturing, safe and loving environment, but rather a home under his control and the control of his addictions and abuse. This feeling of not fitting in, being rejected, and the pain of not being nurtured, but being under someone else's control began a sick pattern in me. It would lead to future codependence and ungodly relationships, where I found myself submitting to ungodly men rather than God. Satan's desire to keep us held and bound is his sick way of trying to destroy the testimony of God's work in our lives and, ultimately, us.

The train passed, the gate opened, and the rescue was finally finished. As Jesus said, "It is finished." This was His plan and His work of miracles. He allowed it for His purpose and His glory. Jesus knew how it would end and why it was so important to rescue me from that town and that family. This was an end to a very bitter and painful life, and it was the beginning to a long unknown road ahead. All I can say is that God knows all and He will cause all things to work together for good for those that love Him and are called according to His purpose (Rom. 8:28).

CHAPTER TWO
RESCUED FROM WHAT?

My mother rescued me from a life of physical and spiritual poverty. She laid her life down to save me and to give me a better life. She did not rest until she had me back. She said that I was full of human feces and my hair was so knotted from dirt and lack of washing and combing that she was forced to cut it off. The odor I gave off was so unbearable that she said they had to stop at a restaurant along the way to bathe me.

Life with my father was not kind to me. It was not what someone would call normal by any human definition. During the time that I stayed with my dad, I learned the effect words could have on someone. They told me that my mother was a witch and that if I went back to her she would kill me. Looking back, I wonder how they could decide for me that life with my father was better. My father was so desperate to drink that he would rather take me with him to the bars than stay home when there was no one to watch me. Their desire to have me was greater than their desire for me to have a good life. The question is, whose desire were they satisfying? Were they putting themselves first, or better yet, who was trying to stop me from fulfilling the destiny God had for me? Did they not know they could not stop the plan of God? No one could! When people tried, they only ended up fighting against God, not man.

I remember the trips to the bars with my father very clearly. I remember sitting on his lap as he drank until he could drink no more. Then, as we walked home hand in hand, he would become dizzy, fall down, and pass out in the street. I was left standing with him in the middle of nowhere, in the middle of the night. I sat with him on the side of the road like a faithful pet, waiting for someone to come to our rescue. There were times when my father left me with his brother's family so he could go on his drinking binge. I remember how frightened I was of them and thought of them as strangers. I certainly did not like to stay there; to me they were animals of another kind. I experienced feelings of loneliness there that I couldn't find words to describe.

I thought of these relatives as monsters because I remember having to hide from their sons in order to get away from their preying hands. The sons were very pushy and aggressive towards me in ways I would rather not describe. I can clearly recall feeling scared, confused, and lonely. At times, I had no choice but to freeze and allow them to have their way, since I was outnumbered.

The spirit of fear flourishes in these types of situations. When a young and innocent child that does not understand life is exposed to the harsh reality of life, the spirit withers and fear latches on with claws that want to kill, steal, and destroy. The eyes are a mirror and fear creates a dazed and cold look that can be seen clearly in a lost child's frightened eyes. As an adult, I remember the feelings that caused these troubling looks. However, knowing what I know now, I can still say that God was with me. The Bible says that angels watch over us. God will never interfere with our choices or the choices of others, but He sees everything.

For he will command his angels concerning you to guard you in all your ways; they will lift you up in their hands, so that you will not strike your foot against a stone.
Psalm 91:11-12

He also has a very harsh warning for those who abuse children or cause them to fall. Perhaps we do not see God's hand of judgment in this lifetime, but nothing will get past Him without being addressed. One day, we will all stand before Him and have to give an account for our deeds and actions because He is Lord of all. The Bible says that every knee shall bow and every tongue will confess that He is Lord (Romans 14:11).

But if anyone causes one of these little ones who believe in me to sin, it would be better for him to have a large millstone hung around his neck and to be drowned in the depths of the sea.

Matthew 18:6

Of course, God is a God of forgiveness. But only He knows the hearts of man and those who truly seek to be forgiven. I chose to forgive them all. In order for my life to go on in God's will and plan, I had to let go and forgive. I believe they did not know any better. They were just pawns in the hands of Satan. I pray someone has had a chance to tell them about Jesus' forgiving love and power. We must forgive in order to free ourselves from the bondage of bitterness and anger, otherwise we will only hurt ourselves and stunt our growth in Christ.

Now, back to the village life. Bathroom ethics did not really apply in the village where I lived. I remember going to the bathroom out in the street whenever the need presented itself. It did not matter, there was no shame, and it felt very normal. Sickness was also very common among children in that area since the living conditions were considered one of the most underprivileged in the country. I remember being very sick several times and once overhearing my father say that he thought I was going to die. But God brought me through it and now, I had a new chance for life because God had put a desire and a pull in my mother's heart to not leave me there. I thanked her for not giving up. However, as I grew, I also saw the need for her to learn to let go and let God take over and continue His work within me. Sometimes, mothers take possession of their children as if they were theirs alone. Although the love of a mother is very special and precious, mothers also have to learn to lay their children down on the altar like Abraham laid down Isaac. We all belong to God, not to each other.

Knowing the end of the story and seeing the difficulties I inherited in forming healthy relationships, I have since questioned my mother's emotional state and her ability to read my needs. At the time of the rescue, she did not know the Lord personally; I became her direct focus of attention. This may have been totally acceptable when I was younger, but I was no longer a two-year-old child. I was now six, and at a different stage of life at this point. However, she was picking up where she left off. In her mind, I was still a baby requiring much attention. As I grew up, I felt like her possession. It was as if she viewed me as a piece of her, and this led to much rebellion.

Since I have given my life to the Lord, I have come to know a true love that lays down its life for freedom, and that is Jesus. He suffered more than any one of us could imagine. He was rejected and beaten and still was willing to lay His life down to die for our sake, so that we would have the chance to be with Him forever. How can anyone turn down that offer and opportunity to be with Him in eternity? He gave us freedom from sin and death and gave us eternal life. The love Jesus offers us is a love we can choose to accept. It is not a love that possesses us if we refuse it.

For he has rescued us from the dominion of darkness and brought us into the kingdom of the Son he loves, in whom we have redemption, the forgiveness of sins.

Colossians 1:13-14

CHAPTER THREE
THE UNKNOWN LAND

I was six years old when I returned to live with my mother. The effects of the trauma in my early years were revealed when it became obvious that I was scared to go anywhere by myself. My maternal grandmother would have to walk me to school. Now that I realized that my mother was not this terrible person that was planning to kill me, I was beginning to feel comfortable and adjusting to life with her, even though the spirit of fear still haunted me. Although we all felt more secure, there was still a feeling that my father would try to come and take me away. My mother feared for me and dreaded having to go through the pain all over again.

When a child goes through trauma, it is common for them to develop mental and emotional problems, fears, and even illnesses. Once again, I became very ill. I went through a time where I would wake-up in my own vomit and urine. I had difficulty keeping down anything solid. I could not sleep and I was

35

becoming more confused as to who I was supposed to live with—my mother or my father. I felt like a stranger in a strange big world. I was having nightmares about my father taking me away from my mother. Living with this type of emotional stress took its toll, and my family decided that it was time to leave the country. Leaving seemed to be the only way to attain freedom, both physically and mentally. But running away from the natural does not necessarily free our minds and emotions. I later learned that only a supernatural healing could truly give me freedom.

Because of the communistic authority in the country, my family had to be very careful how we planned our escape. Usually, the government would not let the entire family leave together. We had to prove to them that we were planning to return. We began to gather material to build a home, knowing all along that it was going to belong to someone else. Friends of the family offered to help us escape and they were also in need of a home, therefore, it was a perfect set-up. We bought the materials for the house and began to build. The decision had to be quick and the plan had to be flawless. Since my mother had a cousin in Innsbruck, Austria, and since the country was close to Hungary, we decided it would be the best place to go. Thus, in September, 1973, we left Hungary.

Leaving was not easy. It was never easy to say goodbye, not knowing when we would be able to visit again. As we drove away, it was painful but we knew it was the only way to go if we wanted freedom.

Since it was common for vehicles to be searched at border crossings, we had all our important documents carefully hidden between the lining and the roof of the car. We knew if the authorities found our documents, they would send us back and we would have to face the government, who would not hesitate to punish us in some way for attempting to leave the country. At the border crossing, they asked us questions and searched the car, but thank God, they never found our hidden papers. My mother told me not to say anything. Of course, the fear in me kept my mouth shut but did not keep it from trembling.

Once we made it through the border and were in Austria, we went to stay with my mother's cousin. The apartment was small and the living conditions were tight. Therefore, we decided to find another place to live. By nightfall we still had not found a place to stay. Therefore, we found a church parking lot and we slept in the car every night for one week until we found another option. With the last of the funds, we went to a restaurant to contemplate our situation. The choice was to either stay and find jobs or go back to Hungary and face the consequences from the government. The restaurant owner saw that we were disturbed so she came over to inquire what was wrong. When we told her about our dilemma, she responded with a smile and told us that her daughter had just opened a restaurant and she needed help. She went on to tell us that there was also a vacant apartment available above the restaurant that we could occupy immediately—who can say there is no God?

I was left alone in the apartment that night as my mother and stepfather went down to the restaurant to interview for the positions. Then the unthinkable happened. I suddenly realized I was alone, and fear came in like a flood and overtook me. I began to scream as if someone was coming for me. Someone came in the restaurant and announced that there was a little girl screaming in the window. My mother immediately knew it was me. The situation was very dangerous because if the police were called, they could send us back to Hungary. In order to prevent this from happening again, my mother found a baby-sitter to watch me while she and my stepfather went to work.

I thought I was rid of nasty people until I met the babysitter. The lady picked me up in the morning and took me to kindergarten class along with her daughter. It became obvious that her daughter and I did not get along. Of course, since she thought her daughter was always a good girl, I was considered the trouble-maker and the cause of all the fights. Therefore, I experienced rejection and anger. I found it difficult to communicate with them due to the language barrier and because I was shy and scared. This caused me to mentally withdraw and go along with whatever they said.

One time, when her daughter and I had a fight, the mother became very angry with me. To punish me, she refused to hold my hand as we walked in the street. Perhaps this was not a big deal for her, but for me it represented rejection and isolation all over again. I began to cry hysterically and could not stop.

The lady must have thought something was wrong with me because I cried most of the time I was with her. But she had no idea where I came from. She did not know my past life.

After about two months, the babysitter told my mother that she could no longer watch me. It was too much for her. Maybe I was too hard to handle. Maybe she saw I was a disturbed child and did not want me to influence her daughter. For a Christmas gift and a farewell present, however, she gave me a gold cross that had a tiny stone in the center. That cross was very special to me. I did not understand the meaning of it at that time, but I knew it was a comfort to me, and I still have it to this day.

After the screaming incident in the window, my mother hesitated to leave me home alone. But I knew I did not want to return to Hungary nor to the baby-sitter, so I promised her I would not cry anymore. During our time there, my mother and stepfather befriended one of our neighbors. This neighbor was home all day, so he offered to check in on me daily and take me for walks. His name was Ibrahim. I remember him very well. From my childish perspec-tive, he was a very tall man with a long beard and a red turban on his head. We did not speak much, but he held my hand wherever we went. We went for long walks together and oddly enough, this man became my friend. He was kind to me and I trusted him. Strange isn't it? A man from a country where men rule over women showed me more kindness than anyone else I met thus far. I thanked God for showing me that there were strangers who still could be trusted. It was obvious he was not of the same race, religion or background. But the kindness and love he showed me was the much-needed comfort that I was longing for.

Since our apartment was bigger than my cousin's, he moved in with us and eventually takeover the apartment once we moved out. It was in this apartment where the nightmares from my childhood began to haunt me. I dreamt that I was being fought over by God and Satan. The dreams were very vivid and real and I did not understand why I was having them. No one ever explained anything to me about God at this point in my life. Somehow, however, I knew He existed. I remember waking up in a sweat with my shirt wrapped around my neck, as if something or someone was trying to choke me. Night after night, I had the same dream. I was too frightened to tell anyone, so I held on to the necklace with the cross that I got from my babysitter.

Was the trauma causing these nightmares? Or was it that the enemy had lost the first round and was attempting another approach? Whatever the reason, one thing was for sure, God was watching over me, and I was not about to be removed from the palms of His hands.

This reminds me of the fight over the body of Moses (Jude 1:9). After his death, the devil wanted to take his body. The battle is still the same today. Except now, the fighting is over our spiritual bodies, and it will not stop until we are gone from this earth. I may not have been dead, but if the Devil had his way, I would have been. He will always try to keep us from completing our course in whatever way he can.

Is it possible for us to be spiritually fought over? I believe it is. I believe that when God has a special call on someone's life, the enemy will do everything in his power to stop God's plan. Perhaps I could not fight for myself at that age, but it is comforting to know that I had someone much bigger and better fighting on my behalf.

In time, we found out that we could not go to Germany or stay in Austria, therefore, we had to make a decision—do we go back or try to immigrate to another country? My mother decided to contact her sister in America. She went to the American Embassy and began the process. It was a process that should have taken a long time, but God had His hands all over it.

Unfortunately, the money earned in Innsbruck was only enough to cover the necessary medical tests and pay part of the immigration documents. There was more to be done and more to pay before we would see any sign of hope. Since time was of the essence, we decided to drive to Vienna. The American embassy was there, and we thought by being close by we could speed up the process. The journey was exciting and beautiful. The mountains were beautiful beyond words. However, once again, our excitement and mood quickly changed as we realized that we had no money left for food or lodging and no jobs waiting for us in Vienna. We began to look for a place to park and sleep again.

As we drove around Vienna, we realized a young man was following us. When we stopped at a light, he waved and indicated that we should follow him. He asked us if we needed help and if we needed a place to stay. We thought he was an angel. It was a miracle from God! We would not have been able to continue our immigration if this man had not come to our aid. It turned out the he worked for a Jewish restaurant and hotel owner who was known for taking in immigrants to help his business. The owner would send this man to the train station to solicit people as they arrived. That day, he found no one at the station, but when he drove away, he happened to notice our car on the side of the road because we had the symbol "H" on it—representing Hungary, and by that he knew we were not local. That night, we followed this strange person to his home, and he gave us a place to sleep and took care of us until it was time for us to leave for America. By the hand of God, this young Jewish man became our friend and our helper. Perhaps he realized that although he was born in Austria, he was still a stranger in a strange land. He knew his true home was in Israel. He took us in, gave us a place to sleep and fed us. God strategically placed him in the right place at the right time. Truly, nothing is by happenstance. We may not see the hand of God in a situation at that moment. However, He is always watching and leading us down the right path so that each one of us will have an opportunity to one day hear all about God's love and have a chance to choose our destiny.

CHAPTER FOUR
THE PROMISE LAND

It had been a long journey since the rescue. Every time our hope faded, God provided someone to help us. It was not that my mother and my stepfather were some Bible-believing followers of Christ. Rather, it was the hand of God. He had a place to bring me, and He was making sure I was going to get there. I did not know Him yet, but He knew me, and it is comforting to know that He was ordering my steps so that one day I would have a chance to hear all about Him.

About a week after we moved into our newfound friend's home in Vienna, we were ready to go to America. We arrived with the clothes on our backs and one suitcase. We could not speak a word of English, and we had no idea what we were going to do or how we were going to survive.

Moving to another new and foreign country was not going to be easy. My disappointments and rejections were just beginning. Here in America, an eight-year-old foreign girl was not going to be greeted very warmly and openly—not in 1975 and not in the area where foreigners were considered the minority.

I am convinced that children do not have to be taught how to be bad or nasty. Because of the fall in the Garden of Eden, we are all born with a sinful nature. It comes natural. The culture I came from was very different, and the children my age did not understand it. I quickly learned that I did not have friends. In their eyes, I did not come from a wealthy family and we did not drive an expensive car therefore, I did not belong. Most of my young school years were spent fighting for my right to be in this land of freedom and opportunity.

The next time I heard about God was from one of my classmates during my pre-teen years. I was always curious about church and God, but never knew how to pursue Him. I was not taught nor did I ask anyone, but somehow, I knew and believed that God existed. God became my only friend in America. When I heard my mother and stepfather arguing, I found comfort in seeking Him the only way I knew how, which was to talk to Him and hold His image close to my heart. As soon as voices rose around me, I would begin to feel very scared and insecure. The feeling of abandonment would come over me very quickly. The effects of my childhood were beginning to catch up to me and I really needed to understand them in order to receive healing. Unfortunately, it would be a long time before anything would begin to make sense.

During heated battles between my parents, I would crawl into bed and pull the sheets over my head and be comforted by the cross I had. It just seemed like the logical thing to do. I had no one else to run to or to speak to about these problems. Perhaps that was exactly where God wanted me. It is where He wants us today. As followers of Jesus Christ, we are to turn to Him and not to others in our time of distress and trouble. Yet so many of us run to others first for answers and comfort when our perfect comforter is right there with open arms, waiting to comfort us.

Come to me, all you who are weary and burdened, and I will give you rest. Take my yoke upon you and learn from me, for I am gentle and humble in heart, and you will find rest for your souls. For my yoke is easy and my burden is light.

Matthew 11:28-30

It always amazed me in my subconscious, how I knew I could go to Christ even though no one explained Him to me. Who can deny that God puts this knowledge of Himself inside of us? Romans 1:20 says that we were born with knowledge of Him that He put in us from the beginning of time and we are without excuse. The dreams I had, the prayers I prayed, He knew about them all. The Bible says that the Holy Spirit moves about the earth seeking out those whose hearts are open. God gently woos us to Himself by His Holy Spirit and we are able to enter in and be in His presence because of Jesus. The Apostle John indicates this:

> *The wind blows wherever it pleases. You hear its sound, but you cannot tell where it comes from or where it is going. So it is with everyone born of the Spirit.*
>
> *John 3:8*

CHAPTER FIVE
SEEK AND YOU SHALL FIND...

God is very specific in the Bible. He tells us not to go to other sources to find out about our lives and our future. He does this for a reason. He knows who we are fighting in this world, and the Bible says that our enemy is out to steal, kill, and destroy us (John 10:10). I thought about what this actually means. To steal—steal what? I believe it means to steal the faith we already have in God. If the devil can make us doubt that God exists and doubt His hand in our lives, he can gain a tiny access into our minds. Once he has a foothold in us, he will try to go for our jugular. "Steal" in Greek is the word klepto {klep'-to}. It is where we get our word kleptomaniac. It means to commit a theft.

We belong to God. We do not belong to Satan. We have a right to choose whom we will serve. I was not at that point in my life yet where I could make that choice, and the devil was trying to steal my identity even before I knew what it was. I believe that our identity ultimately leads us to the purpose God intends for our lives. It is the very reason God has allowed us to be born into this world and this generation. Although the devil was succeeding in damaging my emotions, he was not going to win.

"Kill" in Greek is thuo {thoo'-o}. It means to sacrifice, immolate, slay or slaughter. How does he want to do it? By killing our spirit and soul, I believe. During my youth, I got myself in situations where I became involved in the occult. When we are young and naive, we try anything and do not understand what we are doing and who is trying to get inside of us. Anything that opens our minds up to the spirit world is dangerous unless it is to the Holy Spirit Himself.

"Destroy" in Greek is apollumi {ap-ol'-loo-mee}. It means to put out of the way entirely, abolish, to put an end to something or someone, to ruin, to render useless, to devote or give over to eternal misery in hell—allow me to repeat that... to give over to eternal misery in hell! How can we not see that Satan wants to destroy our lives before we even begin our lives?

All my past dreams of being choked now made sense. If the devil could have kept me isolated in a small, lost town, he might have succeeded in destroying the future God had planned for me. Is it not comforting to know he cannot stop the plan of God? One way or another, God will make a way of escape and in the process, He will train our hands for battle, which will prepare us for the future. It is a comforting promise we can all claim as our very own.

He makes my feet like hinds' feet, and sets me upon my high places. He trains my hands for battle, so that my arms can bend a bow of bronze. Thou hast also given me the shield of Thy salvation, and Thy right hand upholds me; and Thy gentleness makes me great.
Psalm 18:33-35

I knew that God existed, but I did not know much about Him. I saw how He helped my family survive and I saw how He protected me. But why? What was it that He was calling me to be and do? Perhaps I was not yet ready to know.

As an only child, I always had imaginary friends. I had no problem playing by myself. I could keep a whole conversation going with my stuffed animals. Because of this, I did not have a problem talking to God. I just thought of Him as another one of my stuffed animals. This is a good definition of childlike faith. We need to remember that we can talk to God anytime, anywhere, and about anything.

As I approached my teenage years, not only were my stuffed animals put away, but also my conversations with God. I began to experience the usual teenage dilemmas like who was I, what was I to become, etc. I did not understand much about moral values. I just wanted to be accepted and loved, and of course, with that naivety and that attitude I only got in more trouble.

As with most teenagers I was longing to draw my own boundaries at home, in school, and with others. But first, I had to find my boundaries. I did not want my mother to have input in any part of my life. When she tried to give me advice, I would do the opposite and, if she was right, I would never admit it. This attitude caused my mother and me to spend most of our time arguing. I felt that she never trusted my friends and especially my boyfriends. I was very offended by this. I refused to believe that every man was a liar. When I turned eighteen, I made a decision that changed my life forever. It was going to be one of my most emotional experiences since the time I was rescued from my father's village, but it was going to bring me to my knees.

When I celebrated my eighteenth birthday, my mother and I had our usual disagreement about my boyfriend. We were sitting in the kitchen when finally I told my mother that I would not listen to her anymore. She acted like I was married to this person and he owed his time to not only me, but also my parents. She did not like my attitude and said that if I did not want to do things her way, I should get out of the house and go live with him, and that was exactly what I did. I left that day and did not contact her for three years.

When I left, it felt like I was escaping from the trap of a hunter. It was a bittersweet feeling. I had no idea where I was going or what I was going to do to survive. I just had to get away from her. I had to find myself and begin making my own decisions about life. The problem was that I was not mentally ready. I was not properly prepared or trained to be able to make my own decisions or wise judgments. I felt crippled in this big world. When we are not allowed to experience our own failures, or when someone is always there to rescue us, we do not develop the necessary arsenals to survive as an adult. Sometimes, we can love someone right into the hands of the devil. There is no doubt in my mind that my mother loved me. She only wanted the best for me. But there was too much baggage and too many hurts and pains from the past to work through. We both needed counseling.

In some part of myself, I realized that my relationships with men were sick. I caught the sickness from my mother, who admitted to using men for her own benefit. How could she have known this was wrong? She was not taught what the Bible said about marriage. She did what she thought was right in her own eyes. This view of men affected my identity as a woman and distorted my idea of marriage. Was this what God expected of women? What was my role?

Based on what my mother went through, I understood why she wanted to keep me safe and by her side, but did she not rescue me to give me freedom? Was I rescued from bondage to only be put into another type of bondage? I began to feel guilt and condemnation for leaving her, for wanting to find myself. I remembered her suicide attempt and her desire for me to die with her. As I stated before, we need to be careful. I believe that the act of suicide can be hereditary. If Satan cannot get us by using others, he will try to make us become our own worst enemy. In fact, I began to have nightmares again. Like the time in

Austria, I once again felt like something or someone wanted to kill me while I was asleep. I began to feel a very real void inside and after a while, I began to think that perhaps suicide was a good answer. If it were not for the pain, I would have gone through with it. But as I sat in my parked car at a local train station, I prayed one last prayer. I asked God to show Himself to me. I asked Him to make sure that I knew He existed.

The day after I prayed that prayer, one of my friends asked me if I wanted to have lunch with her and her mother. She said that her mother went through similar things as I did and perhaps she could answer some of my questions. Immediately, I agreed, and I went to see her and asked her to share with me what helped her. That was the first time I heard about the saving grace of Jesus Christ. Without hesitation or deep understanding, I wanted it, I received it, and a seed was planted. Although I felt the same, something very big happened that day. The Bible says in Isaiah 55:11 that God's Word will not return empty, but will accomplish and achieve the desire and the purpose for which it was sent. It may not be immediate, but it will come to pass.

Life was great! I had just invited Jesus into my life, asked His Holy Spirit to baptize me, and was ready to return to my normal destructive lifestyle. I did not understand what it all meant. All I knew was that day in 1986, in the living room of another strange woman, I invited the Lord Jesus into my life and I prayed the sinner's prayer. I admitted to the Lord that I needed Him in my life and that I was a sinner and I needed His forgiveness. Interestingly, the first strange woman I met when I was in Hungary was my mother, who freed me from bondage and introduced me to another type of bondage. The second strange woman freed me from bondage by introducing me to the bondage breaker—the Lord Jesus Christ. Unfortunately, I really did not understand what sin actually was. It would be another six years of self-inflicted misery before I would come to understand the full meaning of being a born-again Christian.

I wanted to live for Him, but I did not want to be told that I needed to change. I did not attend church because I did not know I had to and did not know where to go. Things should have changed in my life after that marvelous and wonderful day, but they did not. They did not because I was not ready to let go of my old lifestyle. Something inside of me told me I should, but I was too scared of rejection and loneliness. I quickly stopped calling myself a Christian after someone held up a mirror to me and I saw who I still was. I really was not ready to make a sacrifice for Him. I did not even know how. But the one thing I did know was that a seed was planted in my heart that day, and God never stopped watering it or watching over me as I kept wandering away from Him. He kept drawing me closer and closer to Him by allowing me to get myself deeper and deeper into trouble. No, it was not going to be easy. I was destined to go through more trials. Looking back, I would say that some of them really could have been avoided had I been strong in my faith and willing to walk the walk, not just talk the talk. I was reading the Bible that I was given and I prayed regularly, but mostly for my needs and desires. I did not know how to pray. I am very grateful and thankful to God that He did not give up on me. If it were up to me, I would have given up on me a long time ago.

As time went on, my relationships worsened. I desperately wanted to do right, but I did not have the wisdom to discern that the enemy was after me, especially now that I accepted the Lord. Therefore, I did not see his fiery darts coming.

Life sometimes becomes so complicated that even reading the Bible becomes difficult. What I am about to share, I speak from experience. No matter what you feel, do not stop praying and talking to your Father in heaven. He will help you and He will eventually get through to you. Do not give up. Once we completely isolate ourselves from Him and stop all communication, there is a danger in completely falling away from wanting to follow Him. We can get ourselves in such a downward spiral that we will not desire deliverance. Please do not forget that after we accept the Lord, the enemy is determined to get us to deny our faith. It is a spiritual fight for life. Thank God that when we are young Christians, God watches us closely like a shepherd and continues to pursue us.

One day I picked up the phone and decided it was time to call my mother. I remember being very scared of rejection. I did not know how she would react. I had not spoken to her in three years. I told my mother and stepfather what had happened to me and that I now know what I did was wrong. I did not mean to hurt them, but I wanted my independence. I did not want to be controlled. I told them that I was glad I left home because I was brought to my lowest point and I had no choice but to turn to God. I shared my new faith with them. They were not impressed. I would learn the meaning of Jesus' statement of not being accepted in your own home (Matthew 13:57).

CHAPTER SIX
FROM FREEDOM TO BONDAGE

After three years of being independent, I moved back home in 1989. Although I thought I had my independence, I did not know how to handle my newfound freedom. Therefore, I yearned to go back to what was familiar even though it never satisfied nor showed me who I was.

I thought I was ready to start all over. I asked God to help me. But as much as I wanted to do the right thing, I could not get started. I did not have the Word of God grounded within me. I was still playing on both sides of the fence. I did manage to end my relationship with my boyfriend. Since he did not care either, the split was easy, quick, and painless. Another lesson I learned from these worldly relationships was that God used the individuals in my life to bring me lower and to show me that only He can satisfy my deepest needs and desires. God does not want us living a sinful life or a life that will hurt us. This is why He gave us the Bible. All our life instructions are in there. All we have to do is embrace them. But God will use all our circumstances and consequences to get our attention.

It was not long after I was free from a worldly relationship that I began dating again. I quickly forgot how God helped me and the promises I made to Him. I had a very strong battle going on inside me. Part of me still wanted the world and the blessings from God. I did not take to heart the warnings. In the New Testament, Mark and Paul both warn us about this lifestyle:

> *For whoever wants to save his life will lose it, but whoever loses his life for me and for the gospel will save it. What good is it for a man to gain the whole world, yet forfeit his soul?*
>
> *Mark 8:35-36*

> *Do not be yoked together with unbelievers. For what do righteousness and wickedness have in common? Or what fellowship can light have with darkness?*
> *2 Corinthians 6:14*

In 1990, I met someone through my parents who would become my first husband two years later. He was educated and friends with the right people. There was only one major problem—we had no idea of the baggage we both were carrying.

The Bible says do not be unequally yoked. With God's help, we could have worked through our issues, but without His presence in both of our lives, our relationship was doomed from the start. I can say this because, later in our marriage, my husband told me he was not willing to give his life to Christ, and he cited it as a reason to divorce me.

I proceeded with the relationship even though I was too young, totally with the wrong motives, and against God's Will. Despite all the warning signs and the feeling that something was not right, I proceeded with the wedding with total false pretenses and hopes.

As difficulties quickly arose, I decided that God was the answer to our problems. I was immediately challenged to practice what I preached therefore, I began my search for God once again. I had chosen to marry outside of God's will and calling and because I did not have a true understanding of what a true follower of Jesus Christ was. However, I was about to embark on an experience that would reveal to me the consequences of my actions and choices.

I had never taken the time or effort to become rooted or grounded in the Word of God. I was calling myself a Christian, but was walking the walk of someone who never heard of God. Unfortunately, there are many people like that in the world today. The Bible tells us to examine ourselves, and when the conviction of the Holy Spirit shows us where we are living outside of God's will and calling, we are to repent and change our ways. Our goal as Christians is to be more like Jesus. Our desire should be to live a righteous life and to serve Him. How can we do that and keep living our lives the way we did before we knew Him? We cannot! Either we are totally and completely devoted to giving our lives to Christ or not. To be in the middle is to be undecided. If we stay in the middle too long, we will eventually move in one direction or another.

I began my walk back into the Christian faith in 1993. I assumed that my husband would also follow. However, I soon learned that our thoughts on the subject of church were quite different. He never stopped me from attending church; therefore, I continued my journey in the right direction without him.

Shortly after, on top of a beautiful mountain at a Christian retreat in Pennsylvania, I rededicated my life to God. I had come to realize what it meant to be a real Christian. However, I was now going to learn what a hard and lonely road it can be when our family does not accept our newly found faith. I realized that there was a lot to learn and that I had missed many years of intimacy and growth with God due to my disobedience and ignorance. I was determined not to waste any more time. I was determined to grow in my faith and become what God had intended me to be. Part of my lesson was learning to live with a nonbeliever.

I got back in touch with some old friends who were Christians who could begin to guide me in the right direction and speak truth into my life. I Thank God for putting the right people in my life at the time I needed them the most. God has never failed me in that area. I thank God for the friends that had the guts to tell me the truth about my lifestyle and who even had to keep their distance from me because I refused to change. I may not have liked the feeling at that time, but it was necessary. The Bible is very clear that we are not to continue intimate relationships with those who do not intend to change (1 Cor 5:1-13). That is not to say we should not love them or show them mercy and grace. However, we are also told to pull them out of the fire, if they allow us (Jude 23). We are called to live holy lives and we have no excuse because we have been equipped to do so (Romans 6:13-14, 8:5-11).

The more I learned, the more I shared, and the more I shared, the more I was rejected. With rejection came isolation and then, depression. The thought of leaving my husband entered my mind several times, until I was shown in the Word that it was not an option. The Bible says that we should stay with them that are willing to stay with us so that they are sanctified through us. This, of course, does not guarantee their salvation, but it gives them plenty of opportunities. This is also not condoning abusive situations. Thankfully, I was not in that kind of relationship.

I prayed for my husband and his family diligently, hoping that either by my actions or the presence of God in my life, they would become interested in God. To my disappointment, they began mocking me, which put a strain on my marriage.

Although I was told not to share my faith unless asked, I was encouraged to go to church and to attend whatever event or Bible study I wanted during the week. As time went on, not only did I hunger for more growth, but I also began to see a difference between the lifestyle God was describing in the Bible and the lifestyle I was living with my husband. I was too naïve to see that my husband and his family saw these differences as an excuse for separation. I viewed our differences as a spiritual gap in our relationship, but never thought of it as an excuse to divorce. I longed to share the wonderful revelations God was showing and teaching me. I was experiencing many new biblical truths, and the thought of having to hold back was killing me on the inside. God's presence filled the gap. However, the spiritual emptiness did not go away because there was division in my marriage.

These realities can either make us grow in our faith or cause us to reconsider our walk with God. I have met some Christians who decided not to be as bold or extreme because they did not want to deter anyone in their family from coming to Christ. It is a difficult life to live, but one worth the cost and sacrifice. I say, do not hold back from the Lord, even if you lose everything. It will be returned to you like it was for Job. Only God knows what is good for us. He knows us better than we know ourselves. At the same time, knowing what the Lord said about divorce and about remaining with an unsaved spouse, I did not want to be the cause of a separation by aggressively preaching to him or spending too much time away. Therefore, I considered the cost and considered his feelings.

Sometimes, no matter what we do, the other person just cannot handle the new faith. When God began speaking to me about being totally separated onto Him, I had to make a decision. If I chose to be used by God and go deeper with Him, I was going to have to listen to the Holy Spirit's convictions about certain gatherings, events, and practices. God says that we are to be separated unto Him and be a peculiar people set apart for His use:

> *What agreement is there between the temple of God and idols? For we are the temple of the living God. As God has said: "I will live with them and walk among them, and I will be their God, and they will be my people. Therefore come out from them and be separate, says the Lord. Touch no unclean thing, and I will receive you. I will be a Father to you, and you will be my sons and daughters, says the Lord Almighty."*
>
> *2 Corinthians 6:16-18*

I took God's Word very seriously and yet very cautiously. My desire was not to do this alone, but to be able to share the view with my family. Second Timothy 2:16 says, "Avoid godless chatter, because those who indulge in it will become increasingly ungodly." I saw the necessity for a clear separation from certain activities, but the cost was severe and painful. No matter how hard I tried to hold on to my marriage, I realized I could not force my husband to accept my newfound faith. I could not force him to love me, nor could I force him to live for God. I knew that I was not to argue with him or anyone else in the family who was against my faith. I was to lay down my family as well as my life. I was to let go and let God work it all out for His glory.

CHAPTER SEVEN
SACRIFICES

As I grew, I was challenged to make some serious decisions. As the Holy Spirit revealed to me the areas in my life that He wanted me to change, He would leave no doubt in my mind that a decision had to be made and a step of faith had to be taken.

After three years of marriage, I learned about the real family secrets on my husband's side. I leaned about open homosexual relationships and child abuse that had been passed down to the next generation. As these sins began to surface, I could not hold my tongue any longer. I felt like Jeremiah before the authorities of the nation. I felt inadequate and uneducated about God's Word. But I remembered what the Lord showed me in Jeremiah about speaking His word with confidence:

But the Lord said to me, "Do not say, 'I am only a child.' You must go to everyone I send you to and say whatever I command you. Do not be afraid of them, for I am with you and will rescue you," declares the Lord. Then the Lord reached out his hand and touched my mouth and said to me, "Now, I have put my words in your mouth. See, today I appoint you over nations and kingdoms to uproot and tear down, to destroy and overthrow, to build and to plant."

Jeremiah 1:7-10

The Lord revealed this verse to me one year before when I had to confront one of my dear friends about an adulterous relationship she was having. I felt like a failure when she decided to pursue divorce, regardless of what God's Word said. After feeling as though I failed God, He showed me that it was not up to me to change anyone. I learned from that experience that God's word would either harden or soften the heart, depending on how the individual chose to receive it.

Now I was again given an opportunity to speak. This time, however, I did not have just one person refusing to believe God's Word, but I had the entire family challenging and mocking me for my views. Regardless of the Scriptures that I used from the Bible, they refused to accept them and me. I remember sitting at the table and hearing a still, small voice reminding me of how Jesus must have felt before the religious authorities. Who was I to feel so mocked? Jesus was not only mocked but also physically abused in front of all.

When I shared the truth about Jesus Christ with all my might and to the best of my ability, and I was challenged, ridiculed, and teased by my husband and his entire family. That night, I realized that my husband was changing. He could not even look at me. In fact, after that evening, he hardly spoke to me. My insides felt like they wanted to come out. I just wanted to understand why something so wonderful was so rejected. If I spoke about any other religion, it was not a problem, but when I said the name of Christ, it was as if I pierced their hearts and committed a crime.

My heart told me that something was wrong, but I did not want to see the truth. I did not want to think that my marriage was in trouble. I faithfully prayed for him. The Lord taught me to pray directly from the Bible. Psalm 1 was one of my favorite Scriptures to pray while my husband was sleeping. I prayed that he would become a witness for his whole family. I prayed that every one of them would remember everything that was quoted and said.

Soon, it became evident that something was very wrong in our marriage, yet my husband refused to discuss anything with me. He would continue to tell me that nothing was wrong. It was in our fifth year of marriage when he finally became honest with me and told me how unhappy he was living with a Christian.

The Lord has a way of preparing us for the future. I believe His desire is for us to be prepared for whatever He allows to come our way. He wants us to trust Him, no matter what happens or what we see. He prepared me for the day when I was told that my marriage was breaking up.

I began that day by getting ready to go to church as usual. While everyone was celebrating Father's Day, I was feeling the loneliness of not really having an earthly father. But this time was different. It was 1995, and that morning I felt more heaviness and sadness than any other time. I could not explain it, but I knew something was going to happen. As my friend and I drove towards New York City and headed into the Lincoln Tunnel, I began to cry uncontrollably. Like so many other times, I thought I was crying because I really hated celebrating Father's Day. This time, however, it was for a different reason. As we headed into the tunnel, the Lord spoke a prophecy to me through my friend.

She said, "God is getting ready to bring you into a very dark tunnel of pain and hurt, but know that at the end, you will come out on the other side and there will be light and joy, and you will survive this journey." I did not understand what that meant at the time, but I would understand when I returned home later that day.

When I returned home that afternoon, I felt the need to once again try and ask my husband what was wrong. Finally, he had the courage to tell me that he did not want to be married to someone like me any longer. I refused to accept this. As I stood in the kitchen, stunned by his words, I felt this stream of energy rush through me from head to toe. I was not quite sure how to react. I wanted to laugh and cry at the same time. After what seemed like an eternity, I wanted to say something back, but I began to feel as though we were not alone in the room. I could feel the presence of God. I knew His presence. I felt His presence many times before, but this time I did not know what to do. God knows how fragile we are. He really knows when we cannot take another step without His intervention. And before I had a chance to open my mouth, I heard a soft, gentle voice behind me say in almost a whisper, "If a nonbeliever wants to leave, let him go, let him go."

I felt this peace come all over me, and as if someone or something was actually standing behind me, it felt like someone put their hands on my shoulders. Then, I heard another soft whisper, "Don't worry, I'm in control. Let him go. I have a plan and a purpose for you."

Well, that sounded easy enough. I immediately reacted the only way I thought I should. I threw myself at his feet, begging him not to leave me. Then I demanded that he stay and threatened him if he did not listen. I was not listening to the words that were given to me. I was acting out of my flesh because I did not want to go through the process of abandonment again.

Regardless of what I heard, in my mind I did not believe that my husband had chosen his destiny yet, therefore I felt there was still hope. No sooner had these thoughts entered my mind than my husband pointed his finger at me and said, "It's my choice. I choose to not believe in your God, and if that means I will go to hell, then so be it. It's my choice."

I was speechless. Reality struck and it felt like a knife with jagged edges going into my heart. It was his choice, and in my mind, I could not comprehend that. Was it that bad to be a Christian? Was it that bad to be married to a woman with morals? I was awed at how God knew beforehand what I was going to hear and what I needed to hear in order to be released from guilt. He prepared me and comforted me. He also knew who was controlling my husband, and the devil knew what he had to say, and the devil was right by his side, whispering the words to him.

My reaction did not have an effect on his decision. And so, as if it were possible, I decided to go through the steps of loss and pain very quickly. No twelve-step programs for me, I thought. That was pretty much my attitude with any problem in life. I always wanted to get through the problem quickly and move on with God. I never wanted to be stuck and risk not growing. I also was afraid that if I had too much time to think, I would begin to feel. I did not understand that sometimes we need time to heal. Praise the Lord that He knows us and He knows how much we can handle.

I can now say that this trial in my life was a good experience for me. Not because it was easy, but because I felt the closest to God. I learned trust, faith, patience, and guidance. I really did not have a choice unless I wanted to allow these circumstances to destroy my walk with the Lord and destroy me.

There have been many commentaries written and many opinions stated on the topic of divorce. All I can say is that God is a forgiving God and divorce is not the unpardonable sin. We do suffer consequences from our actions, no matter what sin we commit. And with divorce, sin is always a factor, no matter which party initiated it. I knew the Scriptures enough to know that God hates divorce. The fact that I decided to follow Jesus did not give me the right to cause my unsaved husband to leave me or justify my divorcing him. I had to realize that God does not force people to make decisions. We have to choose for ourselves. However, divorce can bring guilt on the individuals involved. In some instances, individuals have forced the other to choose divorce by making the marriage unbearable. This is unacceptable to our Lord. I learned in my situation that being married to a nonbeliever could be the loneliest life. Yes, the situation forced me to seek God with all my might, but the intimacy that a true Christian couple should experience was never felt. However, I learned to be a prayer warrior and an intercessor for my marriage. I used to pray that my husband would be like David, a man after God's own heart. I prayed the Scriptures for him, as God directed me to do. I thanked God for my situation and for every hurt and pain I felt. I thanked Him for every lesson that I learned and for hearing my prayer, even though I did not physically see the results. I really did not yet understand the power of praying the Scriptures over someone, but with a childlike faith, I would pray them and believe them. I believed that I would one day see the results of my prayer.

Regardless, the following year was one of the hardest. I learned the meaning of what it meant to be one flesh. When someone as close as a spouse wants to separate, whether a believer or not, it feels like a double-edged knife is being pierced into the heart. I do not wish anyone to experience the tragedy of divorce. I had chosen to stay with my spouse, hoping that everything would work itself out. But the pain did not lessen because I had agreed to do the right thing. I was reaping the result of my choices and decisions in life. I was reaping the result of a covenant being broken, and there was nothing I could do but accept it and believe God would bring me though it.

During the next year, I experienced many hard and stressful times. I prayed for deliverance and healing. I fasted and praised Him even in my worst times. I felt closer to the Lord than ever before. One night I cried so much that I did not have any tears left—the emotion was there, but my tear ducts were empty. It was as though God was telling me, "Enough crying, it's time for healing and hearing what I'm about to do in your life." It was then that I felt His awesome presence around me. It felt like the arms of the Father were holding me. No matter what I felt, I did not hold back my emotions from God. He showed me that He honored those times and He understood when all hope is gone.

Many people had advice and tried to offer some comfort. I tried everything from walking around the house claiming my marriage and rebuking the devil, to sprinkling anointing oil on his bed. I praised and thanked God for the trial, and then it occurred to me that if God didn't take away our free will, how could I? I could not force someone to stay against their will.

He chose to leave and there was no magic potion to make him change his mind. That was the reality, and I had to face it. The praises helped me in dealing with the pain and knowing that God was with me through the whole trial. He showed me He was going to bring me through this dark, cold tunnel to the light on the other side. Although it was not the path I would have chosen for myself, the marriage did end in divorce. But I now know that God had a plan.

One of my hardest prayers was asking God to never allow me to bring shame to His name. I told Him that I would rather have Him take me out of this world than turn from following Him. I asked Him to show me what it meant to follow Him, and He soon did.

During this time of my life, I experienced some of my greatest revelations from God. I was working a second job to raise money to go to Israel. One day while driving home on a beautiful afternoon, God spoke to me through His creation and showed me what it truly meant to follow Him. As the sun was beginning to set, I looked up in the sky while driving over a mountainous area and saw a mass of small birds flying closely together. They were in perfect formation. As soon as one turned they all turned in perfect unison. They were so beautiful to watch. Then, God spoke it to my heart. He said, "This is how I want you to be—how I want my Christian children to be. I want them to be in perfect unison with Me so that when I move they move."

This requires us to know Him. To understand Christ's personality and character so that when He says "turn and go this way," we turn without hesitation, just like those birds did. It was amazing.

"Oh yes, Jesus," I said, "I want to be like those birds in unison with you, always aware of your voice and your direction and never doubting what you are telling me to do." Oh, but there is a cost to consider and a cross to bear.

There is joy in the midst of pain. Joy unspeakable and full of glory (1 Peter 1:6-8) is an understatement, however, finding that joy means acceptance of both suffering and pain.

I decided life must go on, and in 1998, I became involved in short-term missions through my church. My first mission trip was to Israel. I had the privilege of going to Israel as a tourist one year prior. Going to Israel not only opened my eyes to the Bible, but also put a desire in my spirit for missions. I fell in love with the people and the country. After having gone there as a tourist and then as a short-term missionary, I wanted to go back there permanently. I wanted God to approve my decision. I wanted it so badly that I thought every Scripture in the Bible was for me and was a confirmation. I had so many Scriptures written down as confirmation that, when I was asked what God spoke to me about Israel, I got confused as to which Scripture really applied. I began to see the need to pray for specific direction from God in order to hear His voice clearly.

Many do not know the voice of God and end up making decisions based upon their emotions. I did not want to fall into that category. I knew my heart was right and that kept me going during the times when

I thought I missed God's direction. God sometimes allows us to make decisions that may seem wrong at the time, but they are not, and only time reveals the truth. He uses everything for His glory and allows circumstances to challenge us to grow and mature in our walk. I believe that I am His living example.

I was convinced that God also wanted me to go back to Israel, so I began to plan to make it happen. At this point of my walk, I was relying too much on other Christian friends to help me make decisions—I knew it and God knew it. That is why God was going to use this experience to teach me to know His voice and how to listen for it. I needed to learn this, and the only way was by experiencing it. From my studies of God's word, I knew enough to know that I had to lay everything down on the altar. I had to examine my motives and be willing to part with everything for the sake of following the Lord's Will. I decided to pray about it and ask God to show me, and I told Him that I would be open to going somewhere else if that was what He wanted from me. It was a hard decision because my heart was set.

During one of my morning studies, I prayed for God to show me what He wanted me to read. The book of Ezra came immediately to my mind. As I began to read it, the Lord began to speak to my heart. He showed me that as Ezra was preparing to return to Jerusalem to rebuild the temple and have the materials provided by nonbelievers, God was similarly preparing to send me on a trip where the funds would be paid by nonbelievers. I was hoping this was Israel, but at that time, there were other countries that were in need as well. The US was involved in the war in Kosovo. In my prayer, I gave God permission to change my heart's desire if that was what He wanted. He would answer that prayer very quickly.

But first, He revealed to me once again what it meant to follow Him. He reminded me of a painting that I once heard described by a pastor, which in turn reminded me of my relationship with God. The picture had been permanently printed on my mind. It is an imprint of which I never want to lose sight.

The picture portrayed a herd of sheep in a field with a shepherd trying to lead all of them in one direction. They were all following each other and the shepherd, except for one little odd sheep. This little fellow was going in the opposite direction, and he had a caption over him reading "pardon me, excuse me…." He was the only one trying to go in the direction of the Lord. All the others were being lead over the edge of the mountain, falling to their deaths. This one little sheep was fighting with all his might to go the other way. He was pushing through the crowd and almost being forced to go in the fatal direction with the others.

What a scene! It put a description in my mind of what it really meant to know and follow the Lord and to hear His voice. It also put a fear in me about being careful whom I followed and listened to. Most of all, it made me get on my knees and ask God to help me follow Him, even if it went against what was considered the norm. That was and still is one of my strongest desires. Before I ventured out on my mission trip, I decided to pray that God would teach me this lesson. Praying and fasting was one of the many good habits I picked up from the few Christian friends that I had, and I am very grateful for that. The following week, I heard a lot about the help needed in the Balkans because of the war and so, during my devotional time at work, I prayed that if God opened the door for me to go, I would go. My motive for doing that was to make sure I was not making an idol out of my desire for Israel.

I contacted the missions department at my church and of course, they were planning a trip to Macedonia. Before I knew it, I was in the prayer meetings and planning my trip. One morning at work, I was reading the newspaper in our break room when the Vice President of our division noticed and commented about the war. He asked me what I thought and I told him that it would be nice to help. He immediately suggested that I e-mail some of the employees and ask if they were willing to support my trip. Suddenly, I had a great awakening. I knew that this man never wanted to hear about God and as far as I knew, he was not openly proclaiming to be a practicing Christian. Right before my very eyes, I was seeing God fulfill what He showed me in the book of Ezra months earlier. Right before my eyes, God was showing me His faithfulness. I knew God was speaking to me and I knew He wanted me to go. There was no doubt in my mind. He made it very easy. I not only had enough money to go for one trip but to go back a second time to teach, just like I read in the book of Ezra. God is so faithful to show us His perfect will if we are willing to listen.

One morning, God revealed another wonderful revelation to me as I was praising Him for His faithfulness. The image of a pear tree appeared in my mind. Recently, my family was given a bottle of a drink from my country that was made with pears. I did not see the connection, but God reminded me how the drink was made. When the pears were small enough to fit in a bottle, they fastened a bottle over the pear while it was still on the tree and when the pear grew and was big enough, they would remove the bottle with the pear inside. At that point, the pear was ripe and ready for the rest of the ingredients. As I visualized this, I began to see how God surrounds us and nurtures us as we grow within the palms of his hands and within His close view. And when He feels we are ready and ripe for the field, He sends us. We are protected and carefully watched until the season is right for God to send us and use us.

CHAPTER EIGHT
THE CALL AND MISSION

The trip was planed for May 1999. Our destination was Skopje, Macedonia. Once we arrived, we wasted no time. We were up early the next morning, ready to pray and work. After meeting for prayer at the local church, we were sent off to one of the warehouses where we packed boxes, separated clothes, and packed and delivered food to various families throughout the city.

The mission trip was very successful, and there was much work to be done. Not only did the refugees need our assistance, but one could see that the country also needed help. The Macedonians were experiencing difficult times, both financially and economically, and everyone was affected, including the church.

At that point, I did not see myself fitting in anywhere in that country. In fact, I really did not want to be there. But, as time passed and I saw the country's need, I began to notice my heart change.

One evening, my group decided to go to a restaurant that was located on top of a mountain in the capital city of Skopje. The mountain reminded me of Mount Tabor in Israel. The road leading up was narrow and the view was spectacular. We pulled into a rest area to view the City. As we stood there gazing at the beautiful night sky, we were quickly brought back to reality that there was a war going on. We saw scud missiles being fired in the air. As soon as one was shot up, we watched the other side retaliate. We were standing there in silence, watching and waiting. The sound and stillness sent shivers through us all. The effects of war could be seen on the faces of everyone. War is no respecter of people.

This trip was very different from my trip to Israel. The work that needed to be done in Macedonia was going to take longer than two weeks. My work in Israel was short-term. In Israel, once our group's two-week contribution towards the building of the worship center was finished, we were ready to leave. Israel was expensive and I needed to find out what my God-given talents were in order to justify my mission. My work experience was in office administration, but how could I be used in Israel? Nothing was opening up. In the meantime, here I was in Macedonia seeing the country's need. It touched me so much that I had to give God my desire to only go to Israel. I stood on that mountain in the still of the night crying and praying, asking God to direct my steps. Why did He bring me to Macedonia? What was His purpose? I knew I had to say it and I did not want to. It was the hardest thing for me to say, but I did, and when I did it, I felt a heavy load lift off my shoulders because I knew now I really had surrendered all. I cried out to Him, "Lord, if you want me to stay here or come back to work here, I am open." Nevertheless, I added, "Please don't forget my heart for Israel."

Before we began our day, everyone would meet at the church for prayer and worship. One morning, just three days before departure, someone that caught my attention came into the room. I had seen this person before, but this time, something was different. We had many new visitors come and go because missionaries from all over the world heard about the need and were sending teams. But this person was local and was very different. I noticed that he kept to himself and did not focus on people or look around. He worshipped, prayed, and minded his own business.

That evening, the church had a guest speaker, and my team decided to stay for the service and fellowship. The service was wonderful, and the preacher was speaking about the call to serve the Lord. As a Christian, there were some wonderful times in my walk where, without a doubt, I knew that the Lord was pulling me. His presence was so heavy and strong that, during the altar call, I felt as if I entered a tunnel and no one was there but me. My vision became narrow and blurred, and I could hear myself breathing. I knew the Lord was pulling me to go up for prayer. I went forward with my heart pounding as if it was going to jump out of my chest and everything around me was fading. When the Lord is calling us with that kind of force, there is no denying the pull to obey. I wish the Holy Spirit would always work that way, so that we could never doubt the pull. Perhaps He does and we just need to learn to pay more attention. The Lord reminded me of Isaiah 30:21, which says that whether we turn to the right or the left, our ears will hear a voice behind us saying, "This is the way, walk in it." This was comforting, but it was not what I was going to hear the pastor speak over me.

When the pastor prayed over me, he was led to make a prophecy about touching two nations. God was preparing me for two nations, he said. He did not know what two nations, but the Lord was going to use me somehow to bring blessings to others in two nations, and he emphasized that it would be more for one than the other. How exciting, I thought. I had no idea what He was talking about, but that would not be the first time, so I hid it in my heart. Soon, however, the excitement and wonder consumed my thoughts.

CHAPTER NINE
GOD'S MASTERPIECE

After the altar call, I was returning to my seat when I noticed the same man I saw at church that morning was also up at the altar, waiting for prayer. During the fellowship that evening, he approached me. We tried to converse, but we realized that we did not speak each other's language enough to carry on a lengthy and meaningful conversation. In his broken English, he asked me if I was planning to come back to Macedonia. I told him I did not know, but if God wanted to send me back, I would come. He introduced himself as Miroljub Stefanovik. I had a very difficult time pronouncing his name, but with the help of another Christian sister, I was able understand it. There was no doubt that we had difficultly communicating, but something inside of me was telling me that I was going to communicate with the man a lot more in the future.

Our group stayed in an apartment in Skopje and my room had the most beautiful view from the balcony. I loved to go outside in the middle of the night, pray, and talk to God. When the scuds where not being fired, the stars lit up the sky. My prayers always seemed to sway back to the desire to go to Israel again and the feeling that God wanted me to give Him that desire and my future. I thought I already had, but letting go of something that was strongly embedded in my heart required me to surrender more than once—at least that was what I was beginning to see. During my prayers the evening after the fellowship, I found myself getting distracted by the thoughts of the man I met. I was upset and frustrated because I could not keep my focus on what I wanted to pray for. I finally asked the Lord why I could not get Miroljub out of my mind. I did not know him, could not really communicate with him, and really did not want to for fear that it was a distraction from God's plan. I prayed that God would remove him from my thoughts completely and if not, then to tell me why.

As usual, the next morning we met at the church for a brief time of worship and prayer. I took the seat in the farthest corner of the room. With plenty of other seats available, I noticed that when Miroljub arrived, he chose the seat next to me. We smiled and greeted each other with a handshake. Immediately, I felt what was like a flash of lightning going through my body, I immediately heard a still, small voice, similar to the one I heard at the service the night before, saying, "This is going to be your husband."

I thought I was imagining things. I thought, *How could it be?* Then as we attempted to communicate, he asked me if I loved Jesus. Thinking it was a silly question, I said with a big smile, "Yes, of course I love Jesus!"

Again, immediately I heard in my heart, "And you also love this man." This was definitely the most frightening experience of my life. Here I was, in a strange country talking to a strange man who I could not get out of my mind, and I was hearing God tell me I loved this man? It was not an audible voice, but it made a heavy feeling in my heart. It felt like my heart was going to jump out of my chest again. I literally looked up to God and asked Him what was I to do—marry this man? Little did I know that God was also speaking to this man.

We spent the rest of that day working in the same factory together and joking around, singing Messianic Christian songs. I was very impressed that Miroljub knew the same songs as I did. The more we spent time together, the more we seemed to be able to communicate better. Since we all exchanged contact information with most of the people there, Miroljub and I did the same.

The third day came very quickly and our good-byes were always with mixed emotions. I was especially feeling mixed emotions about the country and about Miroljub. Things were happening very quickly, and I was not sure what God was doing and what He wanted from me. I only knew one thing, and that was to give everything to God, pray, fast, and wait on Him to direct my next steps. As far as I was concerned, they were all emotions, and everything would be forgotten once I was back in the States.

After returning from Macedonia, I picked up where I left off, and that was finding a way to return to Israel. I was not sure how God was going to do it. I prayed, fasted, and kept seeking His will and direction. Remembering the book of Ezra, I decided to go back and re-read it. I found that there was more to the story.

Ezra returned to Jerusalem. The first time he went as a builder and the second time as a teacher and a priest. I was not sure if God was trying to tell me something. One thing was becoming increasingly clear, however, and that was the fact that there was no physical need for me in Israel. Nothing, absolutely nothing, was opening up for me so that I could go. Some Christian friends suggested I go to Israel regardless. They said that God would provide when I got there. They told me to just have faith. Well, I did have faith, but as a single woman at the time, I did not think it would have been wise for me to go there without confirmation or approval. I was given many opinions and suggestions. It was wonderful to have all my friends try to help me, but I did not feel peace from God and without peace, it was not God. Therefore, my focus went back to Macedonia. I was also realizing that I could not stop thinking about Miroljub. Perhaps it was God's will for me to really see this person again. I needed to find out. I knew that if God wanted us to end up together, it would happen. Nothing could stop the plan of God, especially since God's plan was all I wanted. As I opened my heart to God, things became clearer to me. Since my biggest fear was to be out of His will, I went back to His Word for direction and confirmation. I spent time praying, reading and opening myself to the leading of His Holy Spirit. In the next few months, God led me to many scriptures that reminded me of His faithfulness to keep me and to lead me. This time, the Scriptures were specific and powerful. He assured me that He would reveal His plan to me in His perfect time. These Scriptures became my life-line to God. I prayed them, meditated on them, and believed them.

In his heart a man plans his course, but the Lord determines his steps.

Proverbs 16:9

Knowing what the Bible says about our human heart, this verse comforted me and broke the heaviness I was feeling. The Lord was going to be faithful to fulfill His plan.

The lot is cast into the lap, but the decision is wholly of the Lord [even the events that seem accidental are really ordered by Him].

Proverbs 16:33

For the Lord God is a Sun and Shield; the Lord bestows [present] grace and favor and [future] glory (honor, splendor, and heavenly bliss)! No good thing will He withhold from those who walk uprightly.

Psalm 84:11

He spoke to my heart that He was going before me. Just like he showed the Israelites the way through the wilderness with a cloud by day and pillar of fire at night, so our Lord was my Sun and Shield and nothing will He withhold from those who are His. He knows what is good and right for us. We can cast as many lots before Him as we want, but know that if our prayer is for His will, He will see to it that it is His will that is fulfilled—there is no other comfort I desired more.

> *O Lord Almighty, blessed is the man who trusts in you.*
>
> *Psalm 84:12*

> *"Whether you turn to the right or to the left, your ears will hear a voice behind you, saying, "This is the way; walk in it."*
>
> *Isaiah 30:21*

> *The Lord will indeed give what is good, and our land will yield its harvest. Righteousness goes before him and prepares the way for his steps.*
>
> *Psalm 85:12-13*

The Lord, our Righteousness – Jehovah Tsidkenu. Jeremiah 17: 9 says that our heart is more deceitful than all else and is desperately sick. But, when we give our heart to God, regardless of what we feel, He is able to make it new (Jeremiah 31:33-34). He promises to put the fear of God in us so that we will not turn away from Him (Jeremiah 32:40).

I knew that if I gave my desires to Him, He would be faithful to go before me and lead the way. It also comforted me to know that He, as a loving Shepherd, would only give me what was good for me. I may not always agree with His choice of teaching or discipline, but in the end, I know that it will be good for me and it will bring Him glory.

Everything was indicating that the Lord was going to send me back to Macedonia the same year—1999. But, just like the Israelites, I also had to take a side route before arriving at my final destination.

Before I left for Macedonia, I fasted and prayed before going to my pastor for prayer and confirmation. I asked God to speak to my pastor and use him to confirm what I already felt in my heart about going back. I was also willing to not go if that is what God wanted.

I received my pastor's blessing and approval, and I prepared for Macedonia. Then, just when I thought the puzzle was fitting together perfectly, my mission leader told me that there was no work for me waiting in Macedonia. Therefore, she thought it would be good for me to go to Croatia first and then see what kind of work opened up in Macedonia about a month later. Croatia was not the country I had in mind. How did that country come into His plan, I thought? I was stunned and surprised. Immediately, I questioned what I read and thought I heard from God. However, God knew that I would learn some very good lessons there and from my presence in Croatia, later would meet some people from another part of the world that were destined to cross my path. I went in obedience and uncertainty, but knew God would not let me fall out of His will.

CHAPTER TEN
THE WILDERNESS

My trip to Croatia was challenging from the very beginning. I had too many suitcases. Not knowing how long I would stay, I prepared for every season. That would not have been so bad had I known I had a ride from the airport to the school, but I was only given a telephone number of a contact person at the school. Once I got to Zagreb, the capital city of Croatia, I phoned my contact. I was expecting her to tell me my ride was waiting outside the terminal. To my disappointment and worst fear, I was told that they had an emergency and could not send anyone for me. Therefore, I was going to have to find a bus, buy a ticket to Osijek, and get there on my own. From the sound of my voice, she must have known I was about to cry. She quickly added, "Pray for God to lead the right person to you to help you." She said that this was what she always did and God always provided. This was a good test, right? Wrong! I wanted to go back to the U.S.

Well, I did pray and God did provide, but it cost me a good book. I managed to buy my ticket and find the first bus that would take me to the bus station to catch the second bus to Osijek. There, God had a nice student help me. He had seen the commotion the bus driver had given me because of my overweight, oversize luggage. He noticed the book I was reading, and being a student of foreign studies, he asked to look at it. Noticing how interested he was in it, I told him to keep it. It was one less item for me to carry. In return, he kindly offered to help me transport my luggage to the other bus. Praise the Lord!

After what seemed like an eternity, I finally got to Osijek. It was midnight and I had not slept for twenty-four hours. I was tired, hungry and again there was no one at the station to greet me. After arguing with the bus driver again to help me lift my baggage off the bus, I waited with tears in my eyes and hoped someone would show up soon so I could turn around and go back to the U.S. I prayed that God would really give me a good reason to stay.

About an hour later, someone from the university finally showed up. They told me they were late because someone had shut the gate and they could not find the person with the keys. At that point, I did not care anymore. I thanked God for His faithfulness and protection and threw my arms around this strange person who came for me.

I ended up staying in Croatia for one month. I had the wonderful privilege of assisting the school directors with preparing documents for the opening semester and aiding with the needs in the nearby towns. The needs were great and there was plenty of work for everyone, yet my heart longed to go back to Macedonia. I shared the desire I believed God put on my heart with one of my colleagues. He recommended taking one week and going to Macedonia. He said that if God were going to call me there, He would provide a need. However, I became frightened and I prematurely told everyone that I decided to remain in Croatia for the summer.

God was teaching me another lesson about speaking His unconfirmed word impulsively. We are to never quote the Lord without confirmation. I recalled the prayer I prayed before I left the U.S. I had prayed that I would learn to hear God's voice. Well, in order to know it and hear it, I had to experience it. God was kind enough to teach me the first of many lessons to not be so quick to speak.

We do not always understand why God asks us to do certain things or why He decides to send us where we might not want to go at the time. I would like to share something I learned from one of my favorite Bible study teachers, Beth Moore, in her workbook, *Jesus the One and Only* (Moore, pg. 199). In her Bible study, she described the omniscient knowledge of our Lord and His wisdom in choosing certain disciples for specific tasks. From her lessons, I learned that God sees the whole picture. The truth is that we usually do not see what He is creating in us until days, months or even years later.

In Luke 22:7-23, Peter and John are an example. They were the only disciples asked by Jesus to go and prepare the Passover Lamb. Typically, women were the ones who had to prepare the Passover meal. Perhaps they were wondering why Jesus was asking them to do it, but they chose to be obedient regardless. At the time, they might not have understood why God chose the two of them for the task. However, scripture demonstrates why Jesus invested this lesson in these two disciples. Later, Peter would write:

> *For you know that it was not with perishable things such as silver or gold that you were redeemed from the empty way of life handed down to you from your forefathers, but with the precious blood of Christ, a lamb without blemish or defect. He was chosen before the creation of the world, but was revealed in these last times for your sake.*
>
> *1 Peter 1:18-20*

Peter and John prepared the Passover lamb that day because, before the creation of time, Jesus had picked them out for that particular job. They came to know the scriptures and the power of God's leading through the completion of this service. John's vision in Revelation gives us the full picture of what God was beginning to show him at the Passover supper.

> *Then I saw a Lamb, looking as if it had been slain, standing in the center of the throne, encircled by the four living creatures and the elders. He had seven horns and seven eyes, which are the seven spirits of God sent out*

into all the earth. He came and took the scroll from the right hand of him who sat on the throne. And when he had taken it, the four living creatures and the twenty-four elders fell down before the Lamb. Each one had a harp and they were holding golden bowls full of incense, which are the prayers of the saints. In a loud voice, they sang: "Worthy is the Lamb, who was slain, to receive power and wealth and wisdom and strength and honor and glory and praise!" Then I heard every creature in heaven and on earth and under the earth and on the sea, and all that is in them, singing: "To him who sits on the throne and to the Lamb be praise and honor and glory and power, for ever and ever!"

Revelation 5:6-8, 12-13

I was dreading going to Croatia, but I went, knowing that God was ordering my steps. He gave me enough Scriptures to tell me that I had to put my faith to practice now. I knew that I would see the results in the end.

O Lord, I know the way of man is not in himself; it is not in man who walks to direct his own steps.

Jeremiah 10:23

The evening of the day I decided to remain in Croatia, I could not sleep. I felt such a pull within me like I never felt before. I felt like I made a terrible mistake. I had the awful feeling that I ran ahead of God. I felt a heavy conviction for telling those who counted on me that I would stay because I felt that was what God wanted. They told me to pray about it, and I did, but I did not wait long enough for His answer. The waiting is so hard sometimes, but so necessary. I dreamt of being in Macedonia, and I woke up struggling with the idea.

One of my colleagues again suggested that I go, and that if God had something for me in Macedonia, I would know, and if not, I could always return. This time that sounded logical and was the only answer that bought peace to my spirit.

CHAPTER ELEVEN
GOD'S CALL

When I got to Macedonia, I was told that there was no work for me at the church that I worked with earlier that year. So, I thought that was my answer, but then I was approached by a pastor from another town who needed my help as a secretary and an English teacher.

Before I knew it, I was invited to stay with him and his family. With everyone's approval, I stayed with the pastor for approximately five months. Not to my surprise, this was the church where Miroljub was leading worship. I guess God knew exactly what He was doing.

During my time there, I met up with Miroljub once again. Our feelings for each other were soon confirmed, and we knew God had brought us back together. After announcing our commitment to each other, we continued to pray and fast to make sure the Lord was in every step. I recall Miroljub telling me about the peace he felt during our wedding. He said that he never felt this kind of peace before. He said the best example he had to describe it was a feeling of being held and cradled by the Father Himself. Just before I arrived, God had given him a word:

> *Peace I leave with you; my peace I give you. I do not give to you as the world gives. Do not let your hearts be troubled and do not be afraid.*
>
> *John 14:27*

That was exactly what he was feeling. He also had a very vivid dream about me in a wedding gown standing next to him. When he awoke, he heard a still, small voice say that he was going to marry me. He was so frightened that he said 'no.' He thought it could not be. Why would God send someone for him from so far away? It had definitely been a journey across culture and continents, as well as a journey of faith and learning, but the journey and adventure was just beginning once again. As soon as we conquered one mountain, another one was waiting for us in the distance, each one with its own lesson.

We married on November 12, 1999, and we continued to work for the church until God showed us it was time to return to the U.S. This was all a part of God's perfect plan.

We had to learn how to communicate with each other since neither of us knew each other's language fluently. The Lord worked in remarkable ways. We used our Bibles to communicate. From the time we announced our engagement, not one day passed where we did not make time to worship, pray, and read together. To this day, we do the same, and God has honored our devotion to Him. He taught us how to communicate and He taught my husband English by using a Macedonian and English Bible. To our human eyes this seemed impossible, but with God all things are possible as long as God is in it (Mat 19:26 and Mk 10:27). When the Lord's plan is actively working in our lives, He will make sure His plan is carried out to completion. Miroljub and I had some rough times in the beginning, as every married couple does, but we had the seal and approval of our Lord.

In Macedonia, we had the privilege of hosting some missionary guests from Asia. During their time with us, God used them to give us a message. After worshiping together one evening, one of the guests shared with us how God brought him and his wife together. Not only was their encounter similar to ours, but so were their difficulties. He wanted to inform us that after God brought us through our trials, He was going to use our marriage to bless many in Macedonia and elsewhere. This confirmed the same message we both received from the Lord the night we went up for prayer. Miroljub shared with us for the first time what he prayed when he answered the altar call. He prayed an unpremeditated prayer that he was open for God to send him as a missionary to another country, specifically to America. He did not understand why that country came out of his mouth. He said later that it was the farthest thought from his mind because he did not know anyone from there. He and I did not formally meet until later that evening.

Even with all the confirmation we had during some of our difficult times, I wanted to second-guess my call to go back to Macedonia as well as my interest in Miroljub. I spoke to God very openly asking Him if I had made a mistake. Why would He send this man a wife all the way from across the world? For me, the difficulties were not only with language communication, but also with loneliness. I was in a foreign land and living in a very different culture. I did not realize how "American" I was. I thought being Hungarian I would understand, but even Hungary was different. I knew some people thought we were asking for trouble by marrying under such circumstances.

But the Lord kept reminding me of the picture of the sheep and the shepherd I wrote about earlier. He was teaching me to follow Him and not the crowd. He also reminded me of Matthew 9:38: "Pray ye therefore the Lord of the harvest, that He will send forth laborers into His harvest." I felt the need to look up the word "forth" (Strong's 1544) and found that it meant "to lead one forth or away somewhere with a force which one cannot resist... to cause a thing to move straight on its intended goal." That was the pull I could not resist when I was in Croatia. God would go on to show us later why going to Croatia was necessary.

As excited as I was after that revelation, I still battled over the fact that not all Christians were in agreement with me. This is very difficult to accept for an individual who has always longed for the approval of man and who has been rejected so many times. I would like to clarify that the importance of

knowing God's voice and direction is not only important at the crossroads of our lives, but having confidence and belief that we did in fact hear from God
can affect our future walk with God. In other words,
if I was not confident that my decision to marry and
go to Macedonia was from God, my faith and walk
could have been seriously jeopardized. Our marriage
became a testimony of God's faithfulness and guidance. If I doubted God, what would others think of
God?

Before I left for missions, I befriended someone
who meant a great deal to me. I considered her opinions very important and felt that she knew Jesus in
a very intimate way, in a way that I wanted to know
Him. I know that God put her into my life for a season
to teach me and help me grow. However, God did not
intend me to put her words before His. I needed to
learn to hear His voice and distinguish between the
two.

Through this friendship, I learned that it is very
important to remember that our life experiences affect
how we ministered to others. For example, if someone
with a bad marriage, Christian or not, was asked to
advise someone who was considering marriage, they
would not be able to give a healthy, honest opinion.
That was my experience with this friend. I was not
out of God's will because I was considering marriage
to a believer in Christ, someone who was on fire for
Him, someone who shared the same desires as I did.
The presence of God was so evident in our lives that
we knew beyond a shadow of a doubt that God put
us together. Yet, I received a letter the day after my

marriage from this friend telling me never to contact her again because, in her opinion, I was out of God's Will. Perhaps she believed I was never to marry and I missed my missionary call to Israel. Was it God's Will or was it her dream? I made many attempts to contact her, but to no avail. My heart grieved for her, and my love for her is still strong. My heart longs to share the wonderful experiences we all went through. But another thought came to me, a very serious one. Had Miroljub not been God's choice for me and had everyone turned against me, what would have happened to my faith if the marriage did not work out and I had no one to turn to for help or support? Where are the Christians, where is their unconditional love and forgiveness? Even when we err with our Father in heaven and He finds it necessary to discipline us, He does so with a purpose. He waits with open arms for us to come back to Him and repent. It does not mean we will not suffer for our decision, but He does not throw us away unless we choose to not return.

All I can say is that we need to be careful how we give advice "from the Lord." We need to join our sisters and brothers in Christ in prayer and not judgment, unless of course they are doing something that does not line up with the Word of God.

Everything was from the Lord and Miroljub and I both knew it. Our problem was that we expected everything to be nice and easy. The Lord showed us that with the call comes the cost. There were still some missing pieces to the puzzle, but the picture was partially clear.

As our lives began to settle into place, we felt the need to pray for direction. Miroljub and I knew we needed to return to the U.S. Within weeks, everything fell into place. Miroljub got his visa and papers with absolutely no difficulty. It was happening so quickly that we did not even have time to say our farewells.

One week before leaving for America however, I received an e-mail from a missionary family from the States. They felt that they were being called to work in Macedonia. We had been praying God would send someone, and this seemed to be His answer, so we invited them to stay with us the last week we were there. They told us that they were praying that God would arrange contacts for them in Macedonia, but they were constantly hitting a dead end until a pastor friend of theirs told them to contact a pastor in Zagreb, who then led them to a contact in Osijek that gave them my name. So that was the other reason God first had me go to Croatia. Not only did God use me as their contact, but He also put me in the town where God wanted this family to work.

We are only now beginning to see God's big picture. We are so thankful and grateful for His unconditional love, guidance, and mercy. I kept a newsletter from our church pastor in the U.S. that had a quote from him that greatly ministered to me the love of God during my time of testing. I referred to this newsletter many times in Macedonia. It has become embedded in my mind and engraved on my heart. The letter read as follows:

"The Lord will not allow you to be brought down to despair or hopelessness. He will not allow anything in your life that will mislead you or confuse you. He will do what is best for you – but never in anger. God is not mad at you. He will direct you, if you will give Him your faith, no matter how weak. Trust His love."

(Wilkerson, 1999)

The newsletter was for those who had sinned against God, whether a physical sin or just by not listening to His lead. This was for those who had repented. His Word says that He will never leave us or forsake us. He is always there, even in our mistakes. We are the ones who choose to not respond to Him when He tries to help us and teach us.

During the times I was not sure of His direction, all I really needed to do was to trust Him and His love for me and wait on Him. My faith was so small compared to His love and promises. When God calls us, He will anoint us and consecrate us for His work. This is done by the Lord and for the Lord. We only have to be a willing, open vessel. Miroljub and I both see now that there is no good in us and we are not capable of anything, but we do know that with God's help, we will accomplish His purpose and call while we are here on Earth.

The storms of life are not fun, but they make diamonds out of us. And that is what our Lord wants. He will put us back in the fire until we are pure and beautiful. His Word is proof of His action:

"This third I will bring into the fire; I will refine them like silver and test them like gold. They will call on my name and I will answer them; I will say, 'They are my people,' and they will say, 'The Lord is our God.'"

Zechariah 13:9

He will sit as a refiner and purifier of silver; he will purify the Levites and refine them like gold and silver. Then the Lord will have men who will bring offerings in righteousness.

Malachi 3:3

I love how God uses types and shadows in His Word to illustrate how to handle difficulties in our lives. One of these examples is the eagle. I did some research about eagles to see why God mentions them. Just like lambs and so many other animals, I figured there had to be a deeper meaning. I learned many new and wonderful insights, and one was about the way eagles responded to storms.

Eagles know when a storm is approaching long before it shows its fury. The eagle will fly to higher elevation to await the storm. They wait for the winds to pick up. When the storm finally arrives, the eagle sets its wings so that as the wind picks up, they are lifted up by the wind and rise above the storm. While the storm is raging below, the eagle is soaring above. The eagle does not escape the storm, but instead uses the storm to be lifted higher. That is what Isaiah says:

But those who hope in the Lord will renew their strength. They will soar on wings like eagles; they will run and not grow weary, they will walk and not be faint.

Isaiah 40:31

CHAPTER TWELVE
THE JOURNEY CONTINUES

Where and when does this wonderful journey end? It does not end. This journey of life leads right into the arms of our loving Lord and Savior, Jesus Christ, who sits at the right hand of God in eternity.

Truly walking with Christ means dying to oneself and having the will to be crucified, buried, and resurrected with Him. If someone says that becoming a Christian means an easy life, they are wrong, and perhaps they are not walking in seriousness. Christianity is bittersweet. We may not always like what we go through, but in the end, we will see the reason and the need.

God wants us to know who we are in Him. He wants us to have our own identity in Him. This is how we will stand as rocks in times of trouble. We, as humans, need to learn by experience and unfortunately, that sometimes means great lessons of pain as well as wonderful times of rejoicing.

Looking back, I would not change anything because victory is gained by the blood of the Lamb, by the word of our testimonies and by our courage and patience in suffering that we would love not our lives but be loyal to Christ even unto death – Revelation 12:11. As Paul says in 1 Timothy 6:12, fight the good fight... In the end, my dream is to hear the Lord say "Well done, my good and faithful servant..." Therefore, we are not finished; we are just moving on and growing in the Lord.

For me, I see how God has kept me in the palms of His hand and orchestrated every step of my life after I accepted Jesus Christ. I see how He has taken me from mountaintop experiences to the valleys and helped me to make Him the Lord of my life, not just by words, but also by deeds.

Until 2005, I never really experienced what it was like to be in a valley. I thought I experienced it in various ways throughout my life, and I did. But every lesson has its own purpose. God was going to allow me to experience something that would catch my attention and make me a serious Christian.

It began with a problem in my inner ear. I experienced a vertigo attack in 2004 and then another one in September 2005. This is when fluid builds up in the inner ear and causes an uncontrollable spinning sensation. This usually goes away in time and can be controlled with medicine to some degree. Most of all, it's not life threatening, and although uncomfortable at the time, it did go away. At that time, I worked with doctors who suggested I see a specialist to make sure it was nothing else. On October 29, 2005, I went to an ear, nose, and throat specialist. He checked my ears and said that everything looked normal, but found evidence of fluid buildup inside my ears that could cause vertigo. I realized that the doctor was not concerned about my ears, but he immediately took notice of my neck. He felt my thyroid and determined that I had a very large lump or tumor growing on it. After a biopsy, it was concluded that the tumor was cancer, and I needed to have an operation to remove it immediately. They told us that this tumor had been growing for quite some time and, had it gone unnoticed, it could have spread to other areas.

On November 28, the doctors removed my thyroid and some lymph nodes. This procedure was then followed by a radioactive iodine pill. With the exception of taking a small pill for the rest of my life, the diagnosis is that I will have a normal life and will be free of cancer, praise the Lord!

I knew from the beginning that God was going to be glorified in all of this. It is interesting to note that I have not had a vertigo attack since that time. That is not to say I will not have any in the future. However, I truly believe that God sometimes has to allow certain things in our lives to cause us to respond to Him. Had I not experienced vertigo and worked where I did at the time, I might not have had the examination.

Once we had a chance to collect our thoughts, everything began to make sense. From the beginning of the year, God had been warning us to prepare for trials. Miroljub and I always begin our new year with fasting and praying to seek God's will. In the beginning of 2005, Miroljub felt the Lord impress very clearly that he was to anoint me with oil and pray over me because this year was going to be one of my hardest and most trying years. He heard this very clearly, but he did not tell me until my trials actually began. He was not sure if he had heard correctly from the Lord, but when the trials began, he felt it was time to tell me what the Lord showed him. Since then, we have faithfully prayed over each other. Through this entire event, God has been giving us comforting Scriptures as well as some strict disciplinary instructions.

For example, before the surgery, I was praying for the Lord to tell me what was going to be the outcome of all this, and as I went to the Scriptures, I turned to Mark 4:35-41 where Jesus calmed the storm in one word saying, "Peace be still." That pierced my heart and comforted me. I knew I had to trust Him in this and not allow my emotions to get out of control. Miroljub also received a word before my operation from the Lord to turn to John 13:7, where Jesus told Simon Peter that he did not know what He was doing now, but he would know later. From that point on, Miroljub had tremendous peace about the whole situation. The day of my operation, God pressed upon his heart John 11:4 where Jesus said about Lazarus' death that this situation is not unto death but for the glory of God.

However, one of the most impressive lessons about this has been the question of the seriousness of my walk with God. I was indeed going through difficult times in the beginning of that year. I was not as serious about my 'first love' as before. I had made a vow to God a long time ago to follow Him no matter where He led me and to do whatever He asked of me. In these past couple of years, I had allowed myself to become lazy in seeking Him and I allowed compromise in my walk. God takes our vows very seriously and He never forgets them. Most of all, He never gives up on us because He knows how serious we really are. He knows us better than we know ourselves. He demands total commitment and total submission. This isn't something we don't know, but it is something we tend to forget quickly when we get comfortable in our lives. He demands a life without comprise and a life fully dedicated to him.

Just prior to my surgery, on my way home from work, I was praying that this tumor would disappear and not be cancerous. I was praying for God to forgive me for becoming a lazy Christian when I felt the Holy Spirit say to me, "I will heal you, my child, but will you now give yourself completely to me and stop being a hindrance to the work I want to do?"

Miroljub met me at the bus station and he had a word from the Lord that confirmed what I heard. He told me that he just read about Hannah, and how Hannah made a vow to God to give her child, Samuel, to the Lord if He would only just bless her. Hannah kept her promise. Miroljub asked me if I had made any vows to the Lord that I did not keep. With that, I had my answer.

That evening, as I was reading a biography of a pastor and missionary, God confirmed the same thing to me again. The Lord also spoke clearly to the pastor about her commitment to Him. I turned to the next chapter and read the following: "…For if you don't live to serve Me, you have no reason to live… You are not alive only to receive blessings…" (Shaw, Unconditional Surrender, pg 127, 1986) It became very clear to me that God was speaking to me, and it was time to take His warning seriously. I enjoy reading poetry and during difficult times, God always uses it to touch my heart. This is what He spoke to me during this time,

Can love be terrible my Lord?
Can gentleness be stern?
Ah yes!—intense is love's desire
To purify his loved—'tis fire,
A holy fire to burn.
For He must fully perfect thee
Till in thy likeness all may see
The beauty of thy Lord.
Can holy love be jealous, Lord?
Yes, jealous as the grave;
Till every hurtful idol be
Uptorn and wrested out of thee
Love will be stern to save;
Will spare thee not a single pain
Till thou be freed and pure again
And perfect as thy Lord.
Can love seem cruel, O my Lord?
Yes, like a sword the cure;
He will not spare thee, sin-sick soul,
Till He hath made thy sickness whole,
Until thine heart is pure.
For oh! He loves thee far too well

To leave thee in thy self-made hell,
A Savior is thy Lord!
(Hurnard, 1977)

The surgery was successful and necessary. He did indeed heal me. He healed my heart, my body, and my mind, although sometimes the portion that is cancerous needs to be removed. The lessons that I learned from this experience will never leave me. God will and does allow circumstances in our lives to get our attention, and it is wise for us to listen. We do not know what our future holds, but we do know that He demands unconditional surrender and no compromise with this world. He says in Proverbs 9:10-11, "The fear of the Lord is the beginning of wisdom and the knowledge of the Holy One is under-standing, for by Me your days will be multiplied and years of life will be added to you."

We are to be set apart and separated unto Him. We are not to be like those in this world who compro-mise their lives to be accepted. I believe many so-called Christians have compromised their walk to fit in with the world. It is time to get serious because we live in a time where we don't have time to waste anymore. Life is not about what we get or how much we accomplish for ourselves, but rather what we do for the kingdom of God.

I am so grateful for this trial and thankful to God that He would love me and want me to be separated unto Him so much that He allowed this trial into my life to get my attention. Our Lord is not a tyrant, but rather a gentle Father who knows that His children hear His voice and will respond to His calling. Of course, everything with the Lord has more than one purpose. Not only did this trial straighten out my attitude, but God also made sure that a tumor that had been growing in my body for a long time was discovered and removed before it had a chance to metastasize. The final lesson from that incident also brought my husband and me closer together. We saw even more clearly than before why God brought us together, and it was not to be taken lightly. We shouldn't be hindrances to each other but rather help-mates, just as God ordained from the beginning (Gen 2:20-22). We were born to serve Him and to live for Him, not for ourselves. I can't stress that enough.

May this encourage all to examine their walk with the Lord often, as we are told to do in His Word (Ps. 26:2; 1 Cor. 11:28; Gal. 6:4). May this encourage all to keep the hope and faith and realize that nothing is impossible for Him and He sees our promises, commitments, and the decisions we make in the short life we are given here on earth. There is only one thing that we can do to please God, and that is to surrender our lives to Him completely and unconditionally. He does not care about our education, our sacrifices or how far we succeed in this world; He only cares about our heart and our willingness to serve Him and others wherever He puts us and however He enables us.

When I began writing this book, I believed that we were soon going back into the 'mission field.' However, God had us already on the mission field and He was on a mission to get my heart completely surrendered to Him rather than in a hurry to return us to missions. People are dying all around us, and we need to be focused on the ultimate calling, which is to serve and not be so focused on the details. This does not mean He won't send us somewhere outside of the U.S. one day. Rather, it means that we will flourish and bloom in Him wherever we are at the time. May we serve our great Lord with acceptance and joy. It is by acceptance and obedience that we have peace with God.

I leave you all with one of my favorite psalms— Psalm 18, which describes God's awesome presence and influence in our lives and in the lives of those around us. Take comfort in knowing that he really is in control of everything!

I love you, O Lord, my strength.

The Lord is my rock, my fortress and my deliverer; my God is my rock, in whom I take refuge.

He is my shield and the horn of my salvation, my stronghold.

I call to the Lord, who is worthy of praise, and I am saved from my enemies.

The cords of death entangled me; the torrents of destruction overwhelmed me.

The cords of the grave coiled around me; the snares of death confronted me.

In my distress I called to the Lord; I cried to my God for help. From his temple he heard my voice; my cry came before him, into his ears.

The earth trembled and quaked, and the foundations of the mountains shook; they trembled because he was angry.

Smoke rose from his nostrils; consuming fire came from his mouth, burning coals blazed out of it.

He parted the heavens and came down; dark clouds were under his feet.

He mounted the cherubim and flew; he soared on the wings of the wind.

He made darkness his covering, his canopy around him—the dark rain clouds of the sky.

Out of the brightness of his presence clouds advanced, with hailstones and bolts of lightning.

The Lord thundered from heaven; the voice of the Most High resounded.

He shot his arrows and scattered the enemies, great bolts of lightning and routed them.

The valleys of the sea were exposed and the foundations of the earth laid bare at your rebuke, O Lord, at the blast of breath from our nostrils.

He reached down from on high and took hold of me; he drew me out of deep waters.

He rescued me from my powerful enemy, from my foes, who were too strong for me.

They confronted me in the day of my disaster, but the Lord was my support.

He brought me out into a spacious place; he rescued me because he delighted in me.

The Lord has dealt with me according to my righteousness; according to the cleanness of my hands he has rewarded me.

For I have kept the ways of the Lord; I have not done evil by turning from my God.

All his laws are before me; I have not turned away from his decrees.

I have been blameless before him and have kept myself from sin.

The Lord has rewarded me according to my righteousness, according to the cleanness of my hands in his sight.

To the faithful you show yourself faithful, to the blameless you show yourself blameless,

to the pure you show yourself pure, but to the crooked you show yourself shrewd.

You save the humble but bring low those whose eyes are haughty.

You, O Lord, keep my lamp burning; my God turns my darkness into light.

With your help I can advance against a troop; with my God I can scale a wall.

As for God, his way is perfect; the word of the LORD is flawless. He is a shield for all who take refuge in him.

For who is God besides the Lord? And who is the Rock except our God?

It is God who arms me with strength and makes my way perfect.

He makes my feet like the feet of a deer; he enables me to stand on the heights.

He trains my hands for battle; my arms can bend a bow of bronze.

You give me your shield of victory, and your right hand sustains me; you stoop down to make me great.

You broaden the path beneath me, so that my ankles do not turn.

I pursued my enemies and overtook them; I did not turn back till they were destroyed.

I crushed them so that they could not rise; they fell beneath my feet.

You armed me with strength for battle; you made my adversaries bow at my feet.

You made my enemies turn their backs in flight, and I destroyed my foes.

They cried for help, but there was no one to save them—to the Lord, but he did not answer.

I beat them as fine as dust borne on the wind; I poured them out like mud in the streets.

You have delivered me from the attacks of the people; you have made me the head of nations; people I did not know are subject to me.

As soon as they hear me, they obey me; foreigners cringe before me.

They all lose heart; they come trembling from their strongholds.

The Lord lives! Praise be to my Rock! Exalted be God my Savior!

He is the God who avenges me, who subdues nations under me, who saves me from my enemies. You exalted me above my foes; from violent men you rescued me.

Therefore I will praise you among the nations, O Lord; I will sing praises to your name.

He gives his king great victories; he shows unfailing kindness to his anointed, to David and his descendants forever.

I pray that through this book, all will find encouragement to keep pressing on, moving forward in life and in death with the hope and knowledge that God truly knew us and formed us before time began. Remember, it is His plan and His glory. Open your hearts willingly, and give Him your desires and future. If we are willing to accept His only begotten Son, Jesus, as not only our Savior but also the Lord of our lives, He will open up doors we could not have imagined. If we are willing to follow Him wherever He leads us, He will take us places we never imagined. He will walk with us and sometimes carry us if necessary. He will train us and guide us, heal us and build us up. If only we open our hearts, and if only we believe that He can do it all His way—if only we listen.

Are we willing? Are you willing?

References

Blue Letter Bible (n.d.) Retrieved 2005 from World Wide Web: http://www.blueletterbible.org.

Hurnard, Hannah. *Mountains of Spices* Weaton, IL: Tyndale House Publishers, Inc., 1977.

Moore, Beth. *Jesus, the One and Only* (Nashville, TN: Lifeway Press, 2000), 199.

Shaw, Gwen R. *Unconditional Surrender*. Jasper, AR: Engeltal Press, 1986.

Vallowe, Ed. F. *Biblical Mathematics*. Columbia, SC: The Olive Press, 1998.

Wilkerson, David (March 29, 1999) Cover Letter from TSC Pulpit Series.

Printed in the United States
207610BV00001B/52/A